D1566229

HOOSIER JUSTICE *at*
NUREMBERG

Indiana Supreme Court Judges Frank Richman and Curtis Shake in Germany, 1947.

BYRON R. LEWIS HISTORICAL COLLECTION LIBRARY, VINCENNES UNIVERSITY

HOOSIER JUSTICE *at*
NUREMBERG

Sᴜᴢᴀɴɴᴇ S. Bᴇʟʟᴀᴍʏ

Indiana Historical Society Press in cooperation
with the Indiana Supreme Court
Indianapolis 2010

© 2010 Indiana Supreme Court

Printed in the United States of America

This book is a publication of the
Indiana Historical Society Press
450 West Ohio Street
Indianapolis, Indiana 46202-3269 USA
www.indianahistory.org
Telephone orders 1-800-447-1830
Fax orders 1-317-234-0562
Online orders @ shop.indianahistory.org

The paper in this publication meets the minimum requirements of American National
Standard for Information Sciences—Permanence of Paper for Printed Library Materials,
ANSI Z39.48–1984

Library of Congress Cataloging-in-Publication Data

Bellamy, Suzanne S.
Hoosier justice at Nuremberg / Suzanne S. Bellamy.
    p. cm.
Includes bibliographical references.
ISBN 978-0-87195-281-3 (alk. paper)
1. Shake, Curtis G. (Curtis Grover), 1887-1978. 2. Richman, Frank
Nelson. 3. Judges—Indiana—Biography. 4. Nuremberg War Crime Trials,
Nuremberg, Germany, 1946-1949. I. Title.
KF354.I56B45 2010
347.73'14092—dc22
[B]
                                        2009025714

Hoosier Justice at Nuremberg is made possible through the generous support of the Indiana
Supreme Court.

No part of this publication may be reproduced, stored in or introduced into a retrieval
system, or transmitted, in any form or by any means (electronic, photocopying, recording,
or otherwise) without the prior written permission of the copyright owner.

TABLE OF CONTENTS

PREFACE

When Indiana Supreme Court Chief Justice Randall T. Shepard asked me to undertake the writing of this book, my first thought related to whether enough sources existed to tell the story of the lives of these two preeminent Hoosier jurists. In the case of Curtis Shake, his papers reside at the Byron R. Lewis Historical Collection Library at Vincennes University. Fortuitously for me, in the midst of my researching its collection, the library received an additional trove of Shake's Nuremberg papers that proved invaluable. The Shake papers at Vincennes include correspondence, newspaper and magazine articles, speeches, oral history interviews, and photographs, all of which contributed to this book. In particular, Shake gave some lengthy interviews for which transcripts exist that truly give the reader a sense of the man, including his remarkable storytelling ability.

Frank Richman's family holds all of his papers and was kind enough to mak them available to me for research purposes. Edith Richman kept an incredible dia of her entire tenure in Nuremberg that gave me a detailed glimpse into what t day-to-day lives of American judges and their families were like during that histor time. Richman also kept a partial diary of his experiences in Nuremberg, coveri his first few months there and then filling in later in the year when his wife had accident that kept her from her daily journal writing. Along with these diaries, h family provided me with a limited amount of Richman's correspondence, speeche newspaper and journal articles, and photographs. Richman was a quieter man tha Shake and his written record is smaller, at least in terms of what has survived.

A number of people provided me with invaluable assistance and I am deep indebted to them. They include: Robert R. Stevens, Richard King, and Judge Ji Osborne, all from Vincennes; Curt Shake, Shake's grandson; Stephen M. Coo and Philip M. Coons, Richman's grandsons; William Nixon, who steered me in t right direction in my examination of Indiana Supreme Court cases from the 194C and Chief Justice Randall T. Shepard and Elizabeth R. Osborne, his Assistant f Court History and Public Education, who guided me along the way with resear and editing suggestions.

In March 2008, I presented my research on Justices Richman and Sha at a Continuing Legal Education seminar held in the Indiana Statehouse befo a capacity audience of Hoosier lawyers and other interested parties. Numero members of both the Shake and Richman families attended the session and we recognized publicly by Chief Justice Shepard.

My hope is that this book will revive the memory of Frank Nelson Richma and Curtis Grover Shake, both distinguished members of the Indiana Supren Court and of the American Military Tribunals in Nuremberg, Germany. The contributions to Indiana's legal history deserve recognition and commemoration

BYRON R. LEWIS HISTORICAL COLLECTION LIBRARY, VINCENNES UNIVERSITY

RICHMAN FAMILY

Curtis Shake.   *Frank Richman.*

INTRODUCTION

In the years after World War II, as the world grappled with the enormity of the
atrocities perpetrated by the Nazi regime in Germany, two Hoosiers came to play a
significant role in the American response to the unfolding events. Frank Richman
of Columbus, Indiana, and Curtis Shake of Vincennes, Indiana, both served
their state with distinction as members of the Indiana Supreme Court. Yet by the
beginning of 1947, each had left that position and was ready to begin a new phase
of his professional career. Richman planned to teach law while Shake resumed his
law practice. World events, however, intervened when both men received the call
to serve their country as civilian judges in the subsequent Nuremberg proceedings
convened by the United States to try secondary Nazi war criminals. Richman went
to Nuremberg first in early 1947 and stayed ten months. Shake followed in mid-
1947 and did not return home until the fall of 1948. Both sat on the bench in trials
of leading German industrialists, applying international law according to American

concepts of fairness. It was a daunting challenge to which Richman and Shake responded with grace, competence, and high ethical standards, along with a little controversy.

This work tells the story of how these two citizens of Indiana came to sit on both the highest court in their state and on the bench in Nuremberg. As the older of the two men and the first to arrive in Nuremberg, Richman's story unfolds first, followed by Shake's account. Why the American government selected Richman and Shake to participate in the Nuremberg tribunals reflects favorably on their Hoosier backgrounds and values. For both men their service at Nuremberg was the culmination of distinguished legal careers.

Frank Richman as a youth.

CHAPTER 1
Frank Richman, Indiana Years

In the early 1950s, while in his seventies, Frank Richman compiled his family tree, doing it in his own fashion for his children and grandchildren. He declared his purpose to learn what important things his ancestors had done and whether or not he could be proud of them. Richman noted that his lineage was all from Europe, including English, Scottish, French, German, and Swedish forebears, and that "many had emigrated to obtain more freedom, particularly from religious persecution." Reviewing both sides of his family, he observed that his paternal family had been Quakers in New Jersey, then Methodists in Indiana. Others were Presbyterian or Puritan, with not a preacher in the lot. Richman was proud of his ancestors, declaring them "a brave people," who were "honest, self-reliant, God fearing and God loving . . . by whose example you can mold your lives."[1]

Richman's family roots in the United States date to about 1770 when his great-grandfather William Richman emigrated from Germany and settled in New Jersey. Family legend says that he taught school in Camden, New Jersey, and at Quaker schools in Philadelphia. Little is known of William's wife other than that she wore Quaker garments and may have been of Swedish ancestry. Born in 1800, Enoch Richman, William's son, moved to Decatur County, Indiana, around 1848 where he farmed. His wife Adeline lived to be 101 years old. Their son Silas Tevis Richman graduated from Asbury (now DePauw University), then the Medical College of Indiana at Indianapolis, and became a physician. Later, realizing the insufficiency of his medical training, he attended Northwestern University Medical School in Chicago and graduated with a second medical degree.

Thomas Nelson Baker, Richman's maternal grandfather, served with honor as an officer in the Union army during the Civil War. He died tragically in Indianapolis in 1865 at the age of thirty-four before he could return home from the war, leaving a wife and two young children. Prior to the war, he had taught in a one-room school. Family lore holds that Baker had intended to study law after the war.

Silas Richman married Elma Jane Baker, a native of Bartholomew County, Indiana, in 1878. While pursuing his medical career, Silas moved his family to various towns around the Midwest. While they were living in Columbus, Indiana, Silas and Elma had two children, Alice and then Frank, born on July 1, 1881. The family next moved to Princeton, Kansas, where Richman attended public elementary school. By his eighth grade year, the family had relocated to Chicago, Illinois, where Richman graduated from Englewood High School just shy of his sixteenth birthday. His next step was to enroll at Northwestern University Medical School with the intention of becoming a doctor like his father. When he realized his heart was not in medicine, Richman transferred to and received his AB degree from Lake Forest College in suburban Chicago in 1904.

For the first two years following his graduation from Lake Forest, Richman pursued a career as a newspaper reporter, working in Rockford, Illinois, and then La Crosse, Wisconsin. After deciding that his future lay in the law, he enrolled at the University of Chicago Law School from 1906 to 1908. He left the school after completing all his coursework and being elected to the Order of the Coif, but without the funds to pay for a sheepskin diploma. The bar of Bartholomew County, Indiana, admitted him to the practice of law in 1908 even without the formal degree. In accordance with the 1851 Indiana Constitution, the state at that time did not require any formal legal education as a condition for admission to the bar. In fact, any person of "good moral character" could become a member of the bar. Traditionally aspiring lawyers in Indiana apprenticed with established attorneys for a negotiated period of time until the aspirant gained admission to the bar. This practice lasted until the 1940s when the Indiana Supreme Court finally refused to give credit for legal internships. Nor did Indiana require any kind of licensing exam until 1931, when the legislature gave the state supreme court the right to set its own rules for the admission of lawyers to the practice of law. The court at once implemented new rules requiring the passing of a written examination.[2] Thus, Richman's admission to the bar in 1908 without a law degree or written examination was in no way unusual. In 1940 the University of Chicago waived its fee and finally awarded Richman, by then a nominee for the Indiana Supreme Court, a juris doctor degree, fulfilling one of his lifelong dreams.[3]

The year 1908 was a watershed year in Richman's life. First, he returned to Columbus and joined his uncle Charles S. Baker in the practice of law, naming their firm Baker & Richman. That same year in Studley, Kansas, he married his college sweetheart Edith Elizabeth Rogers, a native of Ottumwa,

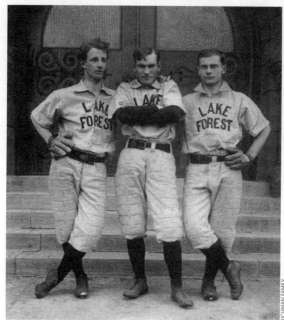

Frank Richman as a young man.

Frank Richman (left) at Lake Forest College.

Iowa, who had attended the University of Colorado, Lake Forest College, and finally graduated from the University of Kansas in 1907. Richman and his wife had four children: Charles Philip, born in 1911; Margaret Louise, born in 1913; Frances Edith, born in 1916; and Elizabeth, born in 1929. The Richman family assumed a prominent role in the civic life of Columbus with Richman dedicating himself to community service. He served as chairman of the Columbus chapter of the American Red Cross for seventeen years beginning in 1922. He joined with others to found the Boys' Club (later the Foundation for Youth), the Bartholomew County Historical Society, and the Rotary Club of Columbus. He also remained active in his Presbyterian church and the Masons.

In 1931, when Charles Baker became a judge of the Bartholomew Circuit Court, Richman formed a law partnership with Julian Sharpnack that continued until 1941, when Richman assumed his seat on the Indiana Supreme Court.

Professionally, he served as president of the Indiana State Bar Association in 1931 and 1932. In 1930, as chairman of its committee on legal education, he led the campaign to rid the profession of incompetent lawyers by requiring Indiana attorneys to have proper training before admission to practice. Known as a man of integrity, Richman's fight for high ethical standards in the legal profession led to his participation in the preparation of bar-admission rules that the Indiana Supreme Court adopted in 1931, which gave the court the exclusive jurisdiction to admit attorneys to the practice of law in Indiana. Richman showed his support for the new rules in an article published in the *Indiana Law Journal*, which argued that the constitutional provision on bar admission (allowing admission to virtually anyone) had been repealed at the general election of 1932.[4] When the new rules requiring a written examination were challenged in court in *In re Todd*, Richman appeared as a friend of the court in support of the new rules, and his journal article was cited in the briefs and the court's opinion upholding such rules.[5]

Throughout the 1930s, Richman continued to engage in the practice of law in Columbus. Widely known around the state due to his many years of practice in both state and federal courts and his leadership roles in professional associations, Richman, a lifelong Republican, announced in early 1940 that he would be a candidate for the nomination as judge of the Indiana Supreme Court from the second judicial district. State supreme court judges, while nominated by party conventions for the judicial districts in which they lived, were voted on at large in the general election.[6] His decision to run came after a series of meetings with GOP leaders in the district and consultation with prominent attorneys in various parts of Indiana. Although Richman had served as treasurer of the Bartholomew County central committee and as chairman of the Columbus Republican central committee, he had never sought any kind of public office. Republicans welcomed his decision because he was well known as a man of great ability, integrity, and experience, and well suited for the judiciary. In the general election of 1940, Richman's bid was successful, and he assumed his seat on the Indiana Supreme Court in January 1941.

At the time Richman joined the judiciary, the political atmosphere in Indiana was intensely partisan. This partisanship ultimately had disastrous results for Richman. Elected governor in 1932 amidst a Democratic landslide, Paul V. McNutt ambitiously set out to reorganize the state government and strengthen his power over the bureaucracy. His executive reorganization bill, enacted by the general assembly in January 1933, resulted in a newly fortified patronage machine with large numbers of state employees dependent on the governor for their continued employment. While Republicans ultimately adopted many of the features of McNutt's patronage scheme (including the infamous Two Percent Club), the spectacular reforms of his term in office (1933–36) left many Republicans feeling very bitter and resentful.

Although his lieutenant governor M. Clifford Townsend succeeded McNutt in office in 1937, the elections of 1938 saw the Republicans trounce the Democrats by taking control of the Indiana House of Representatives for the first time in ten years and winning a majority of the congressional seats. The Republican legislators continued their campaign against McNutt's reorganization of state government, liquor control, patronage, and New Deal policies. The Republicans gained further political momentum in the elections of 1940, securing control of both houses of the Indiana legislature and defeating the incumbent U.S. senator Sherman Minton. Raymond E. Willis, an Angola newspaper publisher, assumed Minton's seat. The only Democratic victory of the 1940 campaign came in the gubernatorial race where Democrat Henry F. Schricker won by a narrow margin.

Not closely allied with his Democratic predecessors, Schricker attempted to work with the Republicans in the legislature by calling for the repeal of

McNutt's state government reorganization act of 1933. Unfortunately for Schricker, Republicans were not interested in compromise. They wanted to reduce Schricker to a governor in name only. To accomplish this, the legislature passed more than twenty bills, including the State Administration Act of 1941, all intent on reducing the power of the governor to make executive appointments by providing that elected state officials (all Republican) would become the controlling members of all state administrative agencies. While Schricker may at first have seemed unlikely to protest these moves, he was not about to roll over at such a blatant power grab. He vetoed the bills; the Republicans, with their control of the legislature, overrode all the vetoes but one.[7]

Schricker took his case to the courts. In the case of *Tucker v. State*, the Indiana Supreme Court held "that the legislative reorganization of the executive branch deprived the governor of his legitimate constitutional authority and violated the state constitution's principles of separation of powers and checks and balances."[8] Thus, the governor had the sole power to make appointments and exercise his executive authority within the executive branch of state government, which included the administrative department. The supreme court was made up of four Democrats (including Curtis Shake) and one Republican, Frank Richman. Richman was the lone dissenting vote in the *Tucker* case. He wrote an eloquent dissent in which he expressed "no approval of the governmental policy of the statutes in question" but rather a concern about "the purely legal question of validity under the Constitution."[9] Richman refuted the principle that the governor has the exclusive power of appointment, concluding that

> the legislature may determine the public policy as to appointing
> power. Whether that power should be concentrated in the governor,

distributed among the executive and administrative state officers, put under civil service regulations or largely restored to the electorate, this court is not permitted to decide.[10]

After the failure of the *Tucker* case, the Republicans' efforts to limit the governor's powers collapsed, and they were roundly condemned by the Democrats and the Democratic press for overreaching. One of the Republicans' few successes related to the partial elimination of patronage at the state's Alcoholic Beverage Commission. The 1942 elections provided the Republicans with a landslide victory and, in 1944, the party continued its rise by capturing the governorship for the first time since 1932 by electing Ralph F. Gates.

While on the bench, Richman wrote the majority opinion for the court in several noted cases. He addressed the question of what distinguishes a guest from a passenger under the Indiana Automobile Guest Statute in *Liberty Mutual Insurance Co. v. Stitzle*, holding that "expectation of a material gain rather than social compensation must have motivated the owner or operator in inviting or permitting the other person to ride."[11] Other issues raised by the statute were addressed by Richman in *Kizer v. Hazelett* and *Hoesel v. Cain* and *Kahler v. Cain*.[12] *Morris v. Buchanan* dealt with a problem of resale after a redemption in a mortgage foreclosure situation; the court held that attorneys may not establish a formal dummy transaction to defeat the power of resale.[13] In *Nash Engineering Co. v. Marcy Realty Corp.*, Richman analyzed the history of the Mechanics' Lien Law and held that a furnisher of materials to a subcontractor is entitled to enforce his claim against the owner of the building.[14] The court clarified the duty of railroads to children in its tracks and yards in *Indiana Harbor Belt Railroad Co. v. Jones*, holding that the owners had a duty of ordinary care to watch out for children due to their possible presence on the property.[15]

Frank Richman practiced law in Columbus until he was appointed to the Indiana Supreme Court in 1941.

While one might assume that Richman had endeared himself to the Republican Party by his dissenting vote in the *Tucker* case that argued for the legislature's having the power of appointment, the party clearly had other ideas. Throughout the 1940s, the conservative wing of the Indiana Republican Party grew in strength, based in large part on opposition to many New Deal programs and to the growing national obsession with Communism. As the events of 1946 would prove, Richman became a victim of this ideological drift to the right. In June of that year, the GOP state convention, held in Indianapolis, became a hotbed of controversy. Former klansman Robert Lyons, who had been one of D. C. Stephenson's lieutenants in the early 1920s, dominated the so-called Palace Guard that sought to control the list of nominees rather than letting the delegates choose their candidates. For the first time in Indiana history, a political convention planned to purge a sitting U.S. senator. The Republican senator in question was Willis, and the plan was to replace him with conservative William E. Jenner. Two other incumbent Republican officeholders were also on the unofficial purge list: State Superintendent of Public Instruction Doctor C. T. Malan and Richman.

Faced with a revolt of Republican convention delegates against Lyons's influence, Gates and state GOP chairman H. Clark Springer pledged that the convention would be "unbossed," but their actions bespoke their words. The party organization wanted Jenner to receive the nomination, and delegates reported pressure from statehouse employees and county chairmen to support the party's choice. Malan bowed to the pressure and withdrew the day before the convention was to start. As the convention opened, Richman and Willis refused to yield.[16]

Why did the party target Richman? What had he done to so displease the party machine that it determined to get rid of him? His sin apparently was to dissent from a supreme court opinion prohibiting a Montgomery County Circuit Court judge from hearing an injunction suit brought against the Alcoholic Beverage Commission in connection with the 1945 liquor licensing law. Reform of the state's alcoholic beverage laws was a top priority for Gates. In particular, Gates wanted to separate political patronage from liquor control. The 1945 law had improved the situation somewhat and Gates wanted no challenge to it. Richman's dissent in the 3-2 decision in *State ex rel. v. Montgomery Circuit Court* stated clearly that he did not disagree with the result reached by the majority in the case, only with "the method by which the result is reached." A second judge, Frank Gilkison, concurred with Richman's dissent.[17]

Many across the state viewed the decision to purge Richman with dismay. On June 13, 1946, the day the GOP convention was to begin, the *Indianapolis Star* reported that seventeen Republican attorneys, claiming to "represent the overwhelming sentiments of the lawyers of this state," had sent a telegram to the governor warning him that "his political future may be at stake if Judge Frank N. Richman is 'purged' from the Indiana Supreme Court for failure to follow party lines in writing an opinion." The telegram cited Richman's honorable and efficient service to the state and urged Gates to prevent a "miscarriage of political justice" and not jeopardize his own political standing.[18] The *Star* also reported that a former president of the Indiana State Bar Association had contended that if Richman had

The Indiana Supreme Court, January 1941 (left to right): Curtis Roll, Frank Richman, H. Nathan Swaim, Michael Fansler, and Curtis Shake.

Judges of the Indiana Supreme Court on an outing at Freeman Lake, November 1941 (left to right): Michael Fansler, Curtis Roll, Curtis Shake, and Frank Richman.

gone along on the liquor case, he would not be marked for the purge. The *Indianapolis Times* reported on the same day that an early joke circulating at the convention at Richman's expense presumed that he would be purged: "You have heard about how Grant took Richmond, today you will see how Gates takes Richman."[19]

The city's newspapers chimed in with their opinions of the anticipated rigging of the convention. The *Star* wrote on June 13, 1946, that "Indiana Republicans have the right to expect a free, unbossed convention." That same day, the *Times* wrote:

> Men who have served their party loyally and against whom no charges of inefficiency in office has been brought will be purged, purged regardless of the fact that they were good enough vote-getters to be elected. But they don't fit in with the long-range plans of the statehouse crowd.[20]

The media decried the disregard for the people's voice in the selection process for political candidates and the lack of initiative on the part of the delegates to challenge this failing.

At the last possible moment, Richman and Willis withdrew their names from the nominating convention, bowing to the inexorable and overwhelming pressure brought to bear by the GOP organization. James A. Emmert, Indiana Attorney General, received the Republican nomination for judge of the state supreme court from the Second Judicial District, the seat that Richman had held. Emmert's election bid was successful, and he assumed a seat on the supreme court in 1947.

In June 1946 Richman believed his judicial career was over. He had previously taught part time at the Indiana University School of Law in its Indianapolis division during the supreme court's summer recesses. In December

1946 Herman Wells, president of Indiana University, announced that Richman would become a full-time member of the faculty with the rank of full professor. His teaching career was scheduled to commence in February 1947. However, circumstances intervened, leading to Richman's return to the bench.

In early January 1947, Richman was sitting in his office at the Law School in Indianapolis preparing for the new semester when the phone rang. Judge Robert C. Baltzell of the U.S. District Court, Southern District of Indiana, was on the line, explaining that a Colonel Damon M. Gunn of the U.S. Army was in his office with a matter in which Richman might be interested. Richman had never heard of Gunn but went to Baltzell's office and heard his proposition. Gunn proposed that Richman become a member of one of six zonal courts in Nuremberg, Germany, organized by the War Department within the American occupation zone to try Nazi war criminals. Richman, Gunn, and Dean Henry Witham of the Law School went to lunch at the Columbia Club in downtown Indianapolis to talk over the proposal. Richman agreed to go to Germany if the university would give him a six-month leave of absence. Both Witham and Bernard Gavit, dean of the Indiana University School of Law in Bloomington, agreed that Richman could not turn down such an offer and that his service would reflect well upon the university.

Only after accepting the appointment did Richman learn how his name came to the attention of the War Department. Professor Fowler Harper, a colleague at the Indiana University School of Law, and later at Yale, had suggested his name. In a speech he gave after his return from Germany, Richman, who called his selection "a bombshell," said:

> The F.B.I. investigated me, Judge Baltzell added his blessing and thus, without an election, without endorsement of a political committee,

without senatorial approval, and with no designation by the President, I became a judge of an international court trying a case in two languages in a court room of the Palace of Justice in the famous old town of Nürnberg. . . . It now seems a long way for an Indiana county seat lawyer to have traveled.[21]

Richman left Indianapolis on February 2, 1947, to begin the adventure of a lifetime.

SHAKE FAMILY

Curtis Shake as a young man.

CHAPTER 2
Curtis Shake, Master Storyteller

A lifelong Hoosier, Curtis Grover Shake was born July 14, 1887, in his grandparents' log house in the southwestern Indiana town of Monroe City to Daniel W. and Arminda Shake, both of whom were also natives of the state. Born in Sullivan County in 1860, his father, a lifelong farmer, supplemented his income by teaching music. His mother, a hardworking industrious woman, brought hundreds of babies into the world as a midwife. John Shake, Shake's paternal grandfather, served in the Union army during the Civil War. Shake's paternal grandmother, Elizabeth Jarrell Shake, was a granddaughter of James Jarrell, a soldier under the command of General George Rogers Clark at the capture of Fort Sackville at Vincennes in 1779. The government of Kentucky gave Jarrell a land grant in recognition of his services, and he came to Indiana as one of its early settlers. A German immigrant, Shake's maternal grandfather

Curtis Shake (back row, center) with his parents and three younger brothers.

Eighteen-year-old Curtis Shake (back row, in hat and suit) taught in a one-room country school before he decided to study law at Indiana University.

William Wyant also served in the Union army during the Civil War. The eldest of four brothers, Shake was the only one who did not choose his father's vocation of farming as his own.[1]

Throughout his life, Shake achieved fame as a master storyteller. Every event in his life had a story attached to it, beginning with his days at the one-room country school that he attended through the eighth grade. On his first day of school at the age of seven, his grandfather promised him a five-dollar gold piece if he would not be tardy or absent a single day of the school year. As Shake told the story, he kept that goal in his mind the whole year, and the day school ended he ran to his grandfather's house to claim his prize. His grandfather took him to the bank in Petersburg, the nearest town, where the president of the bank told him there were no gold pieces available because gold was not in circulation. His grandfather and the banker tried to tempt him with silver dollars, even doubling the amount, but Shake held firm. Finally, the banker went home and persuaded his wife to give up one of her prized gold pieces. Shake claimed to have kept that coin his entire life.[2]

Hoosier Justice at Nuremberg

In the spring of 1903 Shake graduated from the country school after completing the eighth grade. He earned the highest grade in the entire township on the school's comprehensive final examination. At that time, Harrison Township had no high school. Unfortunately, his father could spare only fifty dollars for him to continue his education so he ended up at Vincennes University, living in a boardinghouse and working his way through school by doing odd jobs. The university called itself a junior college at that time. Shake often told a story about how he was so enthusiastic about attending Vincennes that he showed up at 6:30 a.m. on the first day and, when no one else appeared, was disconsolate until the janitor told him to come back at 9:00 when the rest of the students would arrive. Shake stayed at Vincennes for two years, taking courses that would qualify him for a teacher's license. Barely eighteen years of age when he finished, Shake came home to live while he taught at a small one-room country school with about fifty students from the first to the eighth grades. Years later, he recounted that he earned $1.42 a day for teaching school. During the summers, he worked in town for the local newspaper.

After two years of teaching, Shake decided that he wanted to go to Indiana University and become a lawyer. First he had to convince the dean to admit him without a high school diploma. Higher education being less organized at that time, the dean did not view Shake's two years at Vincennes as the equivalent of a high school education; nevertheless, he agreed to treat Shake's teaching license like a diploma and granted him entrance to the law school for the fall semester.

In the spring of 1907 Shake returned to Vincennes and worked in the law office of Cullop and Shaw, earning one dollar a week for keeping the books and sweeping the office. George W. Shaw, a retired circuit judge, took a liking to Shake and introduced him to the standard legal authorities. He was also featured in one of Shake's favorite and most often retold stories. In 1907 one of Vincennes's leading citizens was Jacob Gimbel, then head of the Vincennes department store of Gimbel, Haughton and Bond, which later became Gimbels of New York. One day, Shaw told Shake that Gimbel wanted to see him, but he did not tell him why. Being young and naive, Shake thought to himself, "Hell, I don't owe him anything. I pay all my bills." So he ignored Shaw's request and did not go. A few days later, Shaw asked him why he had not yet gone to see Gimbel to which Shake replied that he had not been told why Gimbel wanted to see him. Shaw explained to him that when a prominent person such as Gimbel asked to see him, he should go if he wanted to get ahead in the world, that one owed a certain amount of courtesy to someone in Gimbel's position. So Shake, as he told it, cleaned himself up and went to see Gimbel, who proceeded to ask him about his plans and about how he intended to finance his education. When Shake told him that he had six hundred dollars saved and that he planned to work at odd jobs in Bloomington to earn the rest, Gimbel made him a proposal that would change his life. In his own words, Shake described it as follows:

> Well, he [Gimbel] said, "Did you ever stop to think that if you're a
> good janitor, you might be a poor student. If you're a good student
> you might lose your job as janitor or carrying papers or whatever
> you're going to do?" Well, I said, "That's a risk you run." Well, now,
> he said, "I want to talk to you." He said, "I'll make you a proposition.
> I'll pay your way through school. You can buy your clothes and
> charge it to my account here in this store and I want you to go like a
> white man," he said, "I want you to pay your bills. I don't want any
> extravagance but anything that's in the line of education, I'll pay the
> bills." Well, I said, "Now wait a minute, Mr. Gimbel, just stop right

there. I haven't got any security whatever. My father's just a poor farmer and I've got three brothers and I can't give you any security." He said, "I didn't ask you for any security." He said, "I would expect one promise from you that sometime if you ever get able, and I hope you will, and you take this proposition that sometime you help some other boy through school and that'll pay the bill. You'll never owe me a dime."[3]

Shake went home and thought about the offer and shortly thereafter accepted it. He bought a small notebook in which he recorded every expense incurred during his three years of law school for which Gimbel paid. He lived frugally and in the end, his total costs came to $1,534. Shake did eventually repay Gimbel in the manner requested but more about that later. He never forgot Gimbel's generosity and, in the years ahead, took advantage of every opportunity to acknowledge his support. At his graduation from Indiana University Law School on June 20, 1910, Shake delivered the class oration. Entitled "The Higher Duty," he dedicated it to his benefactor, Gimbel, "a man who knows 'the higher duty,'" which in Shake's mind meant duty to one's fellow man.[4] After being appointed judge of the Indiana Supreme Court in 1938, Shake sent Gimbel a telegram sharing the good news and sentimentally recalling Gimbel's kindness:

> As I turn over my law practice here to my son on this new year's day and prepare to assume my new duties, my thoughts turn to you in gratitude and appreciation. You are richly entitled to all the pride and satisfaction that you can find in the knowledge that your interest, encouragement and assistance turned the way of a country boy from the path of uncertainty and started him along the road to the highest judicial office in your native state.[5]

The summer of 1907 presented Shake with another opportunity. Doctor Horace Ellis, president of Vincennes University, had been asked to nominate a student to serve as a guard at the World's Fair being held in Virginia, and Ellis offered Shake the opportunity. Known as the Jamestown Exposition, its purpose was to celebrate the three hundredth anniversary of the founding of the first permanent English settlement in America. Shake agreed and left for Norfolk to join the Powhatan Guards, a group of two hundred young men from around the country given uniforms and assigned to various duties at the fair. Among the highlights of his time in Virginia, Shake recalled seeing the Wright Brothers demonstrate their flying machine (which he thought looked like a "glorified kite") and President Theodore Roosevelt reviewing the Atlantic fleet at Hampton Roads, Virginia. All this was heady stuff for a young man on his first trip out of his home state.

In the fall of 1907, Shake finally began law school in Bloomington where he admitted to being just an average student. His distinguished classmates included future Indiana governor Paul McNutt, future justice of the U.S. Supreme Court Sherman Minton, and 1940 Republican nominee for president Wendell Willkie. Of McNutt, Shake said, "Paul was a young Beau Brummel, handsome young chap. Although he became a public servant, became a politician and a statesman, in those days he was more interested in dramatics than anything else. He was in all the college plays." Minton was later elected U.S. senator from Indiana and then appointed by President Harry Truman to the U.S. Supreme Court. Shake recalled that Minton was "on the football team, husky fellow. After he was in his later years, [he] became an unfortunately pitiful invalid but back in those days he was a strong character."[6]

Willkie ran unsuccessfully on the Republican ticket for president against Franklin Roosevelt in 1940. Shake described Willkie as "sort of a long-haired, noisy, more or less of an agitator." He recalled how Willkie led the independents (the nonfraternity boys) on campus for several years and tried to organize them and control elections. Then all of a sudden during the last term of his senior year, Willkie joined the most aristocratic fraternity at the school. Another tale Shake loved to tell about Willkie illustrated the highs and lows of politics and the capriciousness of political admirers. During Willkie's 1940 presidential campaign, he spoke on Monument Circle in Indianapolis before a crowd of thousands including Shake. Some time after Willkie's defeat, Shake and another judge were having lunch in downtown Indianapolis when they saw a man eating by himself. Shake said to his companion:

> "Look over there. Isn't that Wendell Willkie?" He said, "I think it is." I walked over there and said, "Wendell, that you?" "Why sure, Curt," he said, "How are you?" And we invited him over to sit with us. And I've used that to illustrate just the difference between a successful politician when he's at the top and when he gets low. He's been up to Rushville to look after his farm and was on his way back to Washington or New York or wherever he was living. Election was over and he was a defeated candidate, nobody paying any attention to him. So that's what a change a few months had made in the career of a man.[7]

While in law school, Shake met his first wife, Anna Selesky. Born in what was then Hungary but later became part of Czechoslovakia, she had immigrated to the United States at the age of thirteen. A fellow law student, she could speak seven languages. Selesky and Shake got engaged while in law school but agreed that they would not marry until his gross income was up to fifty dollars a month and he could support a family. Shake recalls that he did not want to "marry a partner, I didn't want to marry an office . . . I wanted a wife, I wanted a home."[8]

After they graduated in 1910, Selesky became a leading attorney of the Vermillion County Circuit Court while Shake moved to the mining town of Bicknell to start his practice, paying four dollars a month to rent an office. Bicknell at that time was in the midst of a growth spurt fueled by the coal mining industry. It had a population in 1907 of 4,005 citizens; by 1920, that number had almost doubled. After about a year in Bicknell, Shake's gross income had reached fifty dollars a month, and he and Anna married in June 1911 in the home of her parents in Clinton, Indiana. One newspaper's account of the Shakes' wedding mentioned that the couple returned to Bicknell on the afternoon of their marriage "where the groom had already in waiting a beautiful furnished cottage—and he didn't even forget to have the garden planted." The following year, their son, Gilbert, was born in Bicknell.

During the early years of his law practice, Shake engaged mainly in suing coal companies and railroads. As he described it, the railroads got so disgusted with him and his partner suing them so often that they turned around and hired them. One such client was the B & O Railroad, the nation's first commercial long-distance railroad. Shake also served as Knox County Deputy Prosecuting Attorney and Bicknell City Attorney. After six years in Bicknell, Shake moved his practice to the county seat. He relocated his family to Vincennes in 1916 and formed a practice with his great friend Joseph W. Kimmel, a partnership that lasted until Shake joined the Indiana Supreme Court in 1937. During his first years in Vincennes, Shake served as city attorney, U.S. commissioner for the Southern Indiana Judicial District, and then as Knox County Attorney from 1923 to 1926.

In the early 1920s, Vincennes University, Shake's alma mater, had reached rock bottom financially, and its board of trustees made plans to shut its doors, surrender the charter, liquidate the property, and pay off as many debts as possible. Only about sixty students remained, and its teachers were owed back salaries. When Shake heard about the board's plans, he organized some of his fellow alumni in an effort to save the school. The first thing he did was to pay a visit to Gimbel, a former trustee. He told Gimbel that he thought, with some hard work and organization, the school could be saved. Gimbel was skeptical but Shake pressed on by saying, "If we [could] . . . put that school on its feet, keep its door open, develop it, would you be satisfied that I'd paid my moral debt to you?"[9] Gimbel replied that Shake would have repaid it many times over if he could indeed save the school.

Shake and his group of young professionals organized public meetings and made a general nuisance of themselves. As Shake described it, the board of trustees, to quiet the group down, named him to the board in 1923. With the aid first of a county tax levy and later assistance from the State, Vincennes University remained in business and became a state-supported public institution. Shake remained on its board of trustees for more than fifty years, assuming its presidency in 1945 for twenty-one years.

In the election of November 1926, Shake ran successfully for state senator on the Democratic ticket. Knox and Daviess counties shared one seat. He served with great vigor, earning the distinction of obtaining the passage and approval of more bills than any other member of either house, and coauthored the Lindley-Shake-Johnson Law, which reduced assessments on Indiana farmlands. Although he had only served as a senator for one session of a two-year term, the Marion County Democratic Service Union invited Shake to serve as the keynote speaker at its annual Jefferson Day dinner on April 13, 1927. His speech, widely reported in newspapers throughout the state, decried the lack of Jeffersonian idealism. Shake then proceeded to review first the failures of the Warren Harding and Calvin Coolidge administrations, followed by the situation in Indiana, where he denounced the corruption in the state governments led by Republican governors Warren T. McCray and Ed Jackson. Shake talked about the effects on the legislature of what he called "Stephensonism." D. C. Stephenson, the former Ku Klux Klan head, had a close connection, according to Shake, to Jackson's administration. At the time, Stephenson was serving a life term in the Indiana state prison for murder.[10]

After the speech, the *Indianapolis Times* noted that Shake was being mentioned as a possible Democratic gubernatorial candidate.[11] Newspapers throughout Indiana heaped accolades on Shake after his stirring words, calling him "red-hot" and "outstanding" (*Decatur Democrat*), "equipped with a cutting tongue" (*Evansville Courier and Journal*), "one of the coming men of the Democratic party in Indiana" and "a most pleasing advocate" (*Delphi Citizen*), and a young man whose "stock is above par" (*Bluffton Daily Banner*). All of these papers regaled Shake as good gubernatorial material, an adept speaker with deep convictions for the betterment of the people of Indiana.

Besides the positive press coverage after the Jefferson Day speech, Shake received letters from prominent individuals around the state urging him to consider a run for governor. Shake wrote one correspondent that "this mention of my name in connection with the nomination for governor makes me a bit dizzy."[12] Others praised him as a "Progressive" and hoped that he would be the person to lead the Indiana Democratic Party "out of the reactionary wilderness in which it has been wandering." Shake's response to all who urged him to run emphasized what he viewed as the key issues: "a return to the era of common decency, the restoration of a measure of local self government, and strict economy in the administration of public affairs."[13] He conceded that he would consider the challenge of a gubernatorial race only if the Democratic Party thought him the right person. In the meantime, he intended to adopt a wait-and-see attitude while continuing to represent his district in the state senate.

In 1928, during the second year of his senate term, the Democrats nominated Shake as their candidate for attorney general. The gubernatorial nomination went to Frank C. Dailey, a distinguished attorney from Bluffton in northeast Indiana. Again, Shake received letters of support from several prominent citizens from around the state, including a few Republicans who were disgusted with the strength of Klan influence in their own party and resolved to vote Democratic. By this time, Shake's reputation for speech making had spread, and one Indiana newspaper called him "one of the greatest orators in the state."[14] About a month before Election Day in 1928, Shake resigned his state senate seat to enable the party to name a candidate for senator whose name would be included on the ballot during the coming election. He expressed confidence that the entire Democratic state ticket would be elected by a decisive vote and declared his desire to avoid costing the taxpayers the expense of a special election to elect his successor should his resignation be postponed until after the general election.

On the campaign trail, Shake often repeated his favorite speech, "The Unknown Soldier." Running in a year when Al Smith, the Catholic governor of New York, headed the national ticket, the theme of that address touched on the fact that no one knew the politics or religion of the "Unknown Soldier," just that he had given his life for his country. Yet even that theme proved too controversial for some Republicans in Indiana. Shake would pass out leaflets advertising the topic of his talk without always identifying himself as a candidate for political office and, in that way, attract large crowds to hear the speech. He would conclude the address by reminding his audience that the "Unknown Soldier" may well have been a Catholic and that, had he lived, no one would have whispered that he could not have been president because of his religion. The *Shelbyville Republican* berated Shake for trying to "fool" the voters by stooping "to petty tricks to beguile the people," deeming the

Unknown Soldier "too sacred a subject to be used as any sort of a subterfuge" and declaring that "the attorney-general of Indiana should be above any such action."[15]

Prone to theatrics, Shake joined with Addison Drake, the Democratic candidate for lieutenant governor, to tour the state performing a melodramatic one-act political play, *Civilization Gone to Pot*. This play highlighted the plight of Indiana farmers under a Republican administration. At this time, the Republicans had held the governor's office continuously since 1917. "Drake and Shake," as the newspapers dubbed them, told of places in southern Indiana where schoolchildren had actually fainted from lack of food, "the innocent victims of republican cold-heartedness." Drawing on his early roots, Shake painted a picture of a vast Republican plot to deceive the public as to the true condition of Hoosier farmers.

> Voters driving through the country should not be deceived by
> appearances of farm prosperity. If there seems to be crops growing,
> barns and houses in good condition, with automobiles gracing the
> barnyard, that is merely an optical illusion. If you can run past the
> guards which the national republican committee have secretly posted
> at every barnyard gate, you will see that the farms, crops, barns,
> houses and automobiles are just theatrical properties. Behind this
> painted scenery lie devastated wastelands.[16]

Apparently, some northern Indiana communities took exception to their message. The *Fort Wayne News-Sentinel* reported that Drake and Shake "shed crocodile tears on the best oriental rugs in town in an effort to arouse pity" for Indiana's children. But "instead of sympathetic tears, . . . they received rebukes for soiling the floor coverings."[17] Shake took offense at the lack of respect and unsympathetic attitude shown by the northern press toward the farmers and coal miners in the southern part of the state.

With less than a week to go before the election in November 1927, Shake's campaign received a devastating blow. A fellow lawyer from Vincennes, John Rabb Emison, a former assistant U.S. district attorney and a former judge of the Knox County Superior Court, announced at a Republican meeting in Indianapolis that Shake had formerly belonged to the Ku Klux Klan. As proof he produced a membership book showing that "Curtis G. Shake became a member of Knox County Klan No. 75 on Sept. 30, 1924. . . . The ledger sheet for the year of 1925 shows that his 'dues' together with 'other assessments' were paid."[18]

Emison asserted that Shake received Klan support when he ran for the state senate in 1926 and that, "later, when it became unpopular to be a member, C. G. Shake failed to pay his dues, apparently hoping to quietly lose his membership."[19] He alleged that Kimmell, Shake's law partner, had been a member as well. Emison did not stop there. He made serious allegations about Shake's character, claiming that he was not fit to be attorney general because Shake had defended those who violated liquor laws. Emison claimed that Shake and Kimmell controlled the sheriff, the prosecutor, and other county officials. He noted that the prosecutor dismissed an inordinate number of liquor law violation cases when Shake and Kimmell represented the defendants, arousing suspicion and ultimately leading to indictment and conviction of the prosecuting attorney, sheriff, and a deputy sheriff in a conspiracy with more than twenty bootleggers, most of whom were clients of Shake and Kimmell.[20] Emison asked, "How can any honest, conscientious, law abiding citizen support a man with such a record as has Curtis Shake, for attorney general? His broom in sweeping a clean spot would leave it dirty."[21]

Vincennes newspapers reported that Knox County Democrats planned to scratch their state ticket to vote against Shake's election for attorney general because of his supposed Klan affiliation. Local klansmen offered their personal testimony that Shake was a member of the organization, producing the ledger sheet showing dues paid throughout 1926 as well as an additional sum contributed for the establishment of local Klan headquarters, and what was reputed to be Shake's red and white membership card that he had allegedly lost. The klansmen worked against Shake's candidacy because he had ceased to be a member, joining when it was politically expedient and quitting when it might embarrass him and harm his career. Anti-Klan Democrats intended to vote against Shake due to his one-time association with the Klan. The klansmen appealed to these Democrats to join them in defeating Shake, leaving him in a no-win situation. The *Vincennes Commercial* added fuel to the fire by claiming to have evidence of the "indisputable kind" that the story on Shake's Klan affiliation was true, adding that his partner Kimmel also belonged at one time and had purchased a bond to help pay for the Klan park.[22]

Was Shake a member of the Ku Klux Klan? Only Shake knew, and it is impossible now to know beyond a reasonable doubt. None of the newspapers of the day carried a refutation by Shake of the charges. Nor did he ever directly deny it in any of his surviving speeches, although he often spoke of the corruption of the Republican Party and its links to the Klan. The closest to a denial that he made was contained in a speech he gave in Geneva, Indiana, just prior to the election. In speaking of the unfair accusations made by the Republicans during the course of the campaign, Shake said,

> No candidate on the Democratic state ticket will escape these insinuations and false charges. I have had my introduction to such tactics in previous campaigns. Two years ago, when I was elected to

the state senate, I was accused of having klan connections in Catholic communities and of being Catholic in Protestant communities. The length to which designing and unscrupulous persons will go is shown by the fact that my wife, who is of German birth, was charged with being an organizer of the klan, notwithstanding she was ineligible for membership in that organization according to its published principles.[23]

Years later, when interviewed about the election of 1928, Shake blamed his defeat on the nomination on the national ticket of Smith, a Catholic and an opponent of Prohibition, which is generally acknowledged to have led to the defeat of almost the entire Indiana Democratic slate. Most likely, Shake's analysis was correct, and his alleged link to the Ku Klux Klan played little or no role in the election results. What is known, however, is that the way Shake conducted himself throughout his life contradicted everything in which the Ku Klux Klan believed.

During the ten-year period following his unsuccessful bid to be attorney general, Shake continued to practice law with Kimmel in Vincennes. Their practice focused primarily on representation of the B & O Railroad Company in all its litigation in a four-county area in southern Indiana. Shake stayed involved in politics but from the sidelines where he was often asked to throw his support to Democratic candidates. Very active in civic affairs, he continued to serve on the Vincennes University Board of Trustees and worked (unsuccessfully) to develop two historical sites in Vincennes, the William Henry Harrison Mansion or Grouseland, and the Territorial Capitol, as a part of a national monument project. In 1800 the Indiana Territory was formed with Vincennes as its capital. William Henry Harrison served as the first governor of the territory from 1801 to 1812 and built Grouseland during his years in Vincennes. A Lincoln devotee, Shake succeeded in establishing a shrine dedicated to Lincoln on the Illinois banks of the Wabash River as a part of the trail that the future president followed to Springfield, Illinois.

While practicing law in Vincennes, Shake's reputation for brilliant oratory served him well, and he became a speaker much in demand on topics ranging from local history to Democratic Party causes. In recognition of his success in this arena, the chairman of the Democratic National Committee sent him a letter in May 1936 stating, "A number of prominent friends of the Administration have suggested to me that you could be of considerable aid to the party as a speaker during the coming campaign either for our national bureau or for some of the State bureaus." Shake also published several books, writing primarily about his favorite topics, the city of Vincennes, its university, and other local landmarks. His works during that time period include: *History of Vincennes University* (1928), *The First Capitol of Indiana Territory, 1800–1813 and of the District of Louisiana, 1804–1805* (1934), *The Old Vincennes Cathedral and Its Environs* (1934), and *A Naval History of Vincennes* (1936).

While Shake remained busy writing, speaking, and practicing law, he continued to look for ways to serve his state. On December 12, 1937, the front page of the *Indianapolis Star* carried a prominent article about President Franklin Roosevelt's appointment of Indiana Supreme Court Judge Walter E. Treanor to the U.S. Court of Appeals for the Seventh Circuit in Chicago. Treanor represented the First District on the Indiana Supreme Court, the same district that encompassed Vincennes. As Shake told the story, he had bought the newspaper that day and seen the story about Treanor. He told his partner, Kimmel, "I'm about through with politics, but here's one job that I wouldn't mind having."[24] Kimmel encouraged him to apply although Shake felt sure that Governor M. Clifford Townsend, a Democrat, would already have

SHAKE FAMILY

Curtis Shake at the time of his appointment to the Indiana Supreme Court, 1938.

chosen a candidate to replace Treanor. Shake spent the next day mulling over the possibility and finally decided to write the governor a letter. He knew Townsend casually, the governor having been a Democratic candidate for Congress in the campaign of 1928 in which Shake had run for attorney general. Shake's letter advised Townsend of his interest in the position of judge, reviewed his qualifications, and pointed out that while Knox County voters had contributed to recent Democratic successes, "the county has not been recognized with a place on the state ticket, or with a major appointment since our party came into power in Indiana [1933]."[25]

Two days later, Shake's phone rang and the governor's secretary requested that he come up to Indianapolis to meet with the governor the next morning. When Shake arrived at the statehouse, he was immediately ushered in to the governor's office. Townsend promptly informed Shake that he had already signed the commission appointing him to the Supreme Court of Indiana. Years later, Shake recalled that his swollen head did not last long. Shortly after joining the court, the governor told him why he had been chosen over two other candidates, both circuit judges. In Shake's words, the governor told him, "If I had appointed either one . . . I'd had a vacancy in that county and I learned the hard way it's easier to appoint a Supreme Court judge than it is a circuit judge 'cause then I'd have had all kinds of trouble in those counties. And you came along. You weren't holding any public office and didn't make any vacancies and that's how you got the appointment."[26] An interesting sidebar to Shake's application is that Townsend received a glowing letter of recommendation from Ewing Emison, law partner and brother of John Rabb Emison, who had done so much to cause Shake's defeat in 1928.

After finishing the remaining year of Treanor's term, Shake was elected in his own right in 1938 to a six-year term on the supreme court, a post he held until 1945. He served as Chief Justice three times—in 1939, 1941, and 1944. Along with his judicial duties, Shake became involved on a national basis with the mediation of labor disputes. During the period 1938 to 1946, he mediated approximately four hundred labor clashes as a referee for the National Mediation Board. He served on six presidential emergency boards for the settlement of railroad strikes, chairing three of them, from 1944 to 1947, gaining a national reputation in the process.

Shake wrote several significant opinions during his term on the Indiana Supreme Court. Perhaps the most important was *Warren v. Indiana Telephone Company*, which finally resolved a long-simmering debate over the role of the Indiana Appellate Court.[27] Throughout the state's history, the legislature had on occasion made the appellate court the court of last resort in certain types of cases, thus weakening the state supreme court's ability to shape guiding legal principles. In the *Warren* case, Shake spoke for the court when he rejected the legislature's ability to limit the supreme court's powers of review based on the need for consistency in interpretation of the state's laws:

> Uniformity in the interpretation and application of the law is the
> keystone of our system of jurisprudence. . . . [I]t was the positive

intention of the framers of our Constitution that the laws of this state should be general and uniform so far as it is possible to make them so. Such uniformity cannot be attained or preserved if the courts that interpret and apply the laws are not required to take their controlling precedents from some common source. If other courts than this court are to be permitted to construe statutes and state rules of substantive law, without recourse being provided for review by this court, the result will be as destructive to uniformity as if the Legislature was permitted to enact local and special laws for every county in the state.[28]

The ruling in *Warren* put Indiana in line with the majority rule in the rest of the nation.

Other noted opinions in which Shake spoke for the court include: *Helms v. American Security Co.*, which upheld the rights of innocent purchasers of mortgaged goods where the mortgagee allows the mortgagor to continue to offer the goods for sale in the normal course of business;[29] *Railway Express Agency v. Bonnell*, limiting the liability of the *respondeat superior* where the principal had no right to control the injurious act;[30] and *Heiny, Admx. v. Pennsylvania Railroad Co.*, in which the court interpreted a statute requiring a driver of explosives or flammable materials to stop the vehicle to make certain that no train is approaching, the court holding that the standard of ordinary care—not the statute—was the correct measure of the driver's conduct.[31]

When his term on the bench expired in the beginning of 1945, Shake returned home to Vincennes and the practice of law with his son Gilbert. When asked why he had chosen not to run for re-election, Shake explained that, although he enjoyed the work of a judge very much, he had seen the handwriting on the wall. Three Democratic judges (Shake, H. Nathan Swaim, and Michael L. Fansler) were up for re-election in 1944, and he believed that the state would clearly go Republican in the November election. Wanting to avoid the stigma of being a defeated candidate, he chose not to seek another term. Swaim and Fansler both ran and lost, so Shake had correctly divined the direction of the political winds in Indiana.

One morning in 1947, Shake received a long telegram at his Vincennes office from Washington, D.C. It asked him if he would accept an appointment to the war crimes trials in Nuremberg. Shake confessed that, at the time, he did not know much about the trials other than what he had read in the newspaper. Here's how he explained what happened next.

> So I told the girl in the office, I said, "Don't make any appointments for me. I'm going to the public library." So I went down to the library and I said, "Dig me out what you can about the war crimes." And I suffered from indecision. I'd make up my mind in one minute that I might go and the next one I'd better not. I had a twenty-four hour limit to finally make the answer. Well, the last decision was, I said, "Yes," and I went.[32]

Shake always believed that the suggestion of his name had come from Professor Fowler Harper of the Indiana University School of Law and an adviser to President Harry Truman, the same person who had recommended Frank Richman for his appointment to Nuremberg. Richman claimed, however, that it was he who had suggested Shake's name to Colonel Damon M. Gunn, and he noted in his diary on April 14, 1947, that he had written to Shake urging him to accept the appointment after learning of Shake's reluctance. Sadly, Anna had died on November 2, 1946, so Shake left for Germany alone and on his own.

Frank Richman and Curtis Shake (front row, third and fourth from the right) with some of the judges at Nuremberg.

CHAPTER 3

Richman at Nuremberg

When Frank Richman received his appointment to Nuremberg in early 1947, the International Military Tribunal (IMT) at Nuremberg had already concluded its task of trying the major war criminals of the European Axis. Twenty-two leading Nazi figures had been tried at trials lasting over ten months; all but three had been convicted of one or more of the following charges: preparations for a war of aggression, crimes against peace, war crimes, and crimes against humanity. The IMT had consisted of judges from four countries: Great Britain, the United States, France, and the Soviet Union. As originally conceived, a second international tribunal was to concentrate primarily on the actions of German industrialists and financiers. However, the second IMT never happened. Because of misgivings about the intentions and demeanor of the Soviet prosecutors and disagreements within the American military leadership, the United States chose to go it alone and hold separate prosecutions. Ultimately, each of the four Allied powers initiated its own criminal proceedings against German nationals and held military trials under the provisions of Allied Control Council Law No. 10, which authorized the establishment of the separate tribunals. The American trials, known as the "Trials of War Criminals" or the "Subsequent Proceedings" under the direction of Brigadier General Telford Taylor as U.S. Chief of Counsel for War Crimes, comprised twelve cases against a total of 185 defendants. Those charged included concentration camp doctors, industrialists, Nazi judges, and murder squads.

The American military set up six zonal courts in Nuremberg to conduct the Subsequent Proceedings within the American occupation zone in Germany. Why Nuremberg? In 1934 Adolf Hitler chose the city as the site of the Nazis' annual party rallies. It was also the place where in 1935 the Nuremberg Laws had stripped Jews of German citizenship. The victorious Allies thus chose Nuremberg for the tribunals as a symbol of the Third Reich.[1] Three trials of industrialists were scheduled to take place—primarily against Friedrich Flick, Carl Krauch (head of I. G. Farben), and Gustav Krupp. Richman's appointment was to Tribunal IV to hear case five against Flick and his business associates, known as the "Flick case," the first of the cases brought against German industrialists.

At the time, many viewed proving the charges against the industrialists as the most difficult of all the Subsequent Proceedings. The theory behind the trials of the industrialists and financiers was that they were the men who had "pulled the strings behind the Nazi regime, brought it to power, profited by it, and were fundamentally responsible for its aggressions and other crimes." In part due to the vestiges of feudalism still existing in German society in the mid-1800s, German industry had developed differently from its American counterpart that faced limitations imposed by democratic processes and legislation such as the Sherman Anti-Trust Act. The economic, political, and military power exercised by German big business far exceeded any such power in the United States. The American prosecutors decided not to try and prove that the manufacture of arms in and of itself was a criminal act. Instead, the decision was made to focus on the social and moral responsibility of these companies within the constraints of international law to know the purposes for which the arms were to be used. They intended to prove that the German industrialists knowingly made arms for criminal purposes.[2]

While the six courts were denominated American Military Tribunals and American civilian judges chosen by the U.S. Army manned them, the courts acted under the international law and procedures established by the IMT. Like most of the other thirty-two judges, Richman came from a state court background, not from the federal judiciary. Due to criticism of Justice Robert H. Jackson's lengthy absence from the U.S. Supreme Court during the IMT, the Chief Justice had decided not to release federal judges for this task, prompting criticism by some that the judges selected were inadequate.[3] About half of the judges hailed from state courts of last resort, one-third were trial judges, and the remainder had no previous judicial experience. All were men past the age of forty, split about evenly between Republicans and Democrats and came from all parts of the country.

On February 2, 1947, Richmond left Indianapolis by train headed for Washington, D.C., where he went through a battery of tests and interviews to prepare for his overseas assignment. While in the nation's capital, Richmond saw an old friend from Columbus, Indiana, who was working in Washington. In a prescient foretelling of the McCarthy era looming on the horizon and an indicator of his own moral bent, Richman wrote in a letter to his law partner Julian Sharpnack:

Don looks well, still enjoys his work and despite some of the local residents who have him classed as a Communist is just as sound as he always was. It peeves me to have friends whose Americanism can not be challenged traduced by mossbacks whose minds are closed. I suppose because I have them for friends I'll be put in the same category with them.[4]

A few days later, he met his wife Edith and daughter Elizabeth in New York, along with Jean McGrew who hailed from New Castle, Indiana. McGrew had served Richman as his secretary during his tenure on the Indiana Supreme Court, and she accompanied him to Nuremberg to work in a similar capacity. After staying a few days at Fort Hamilton in Brooklyn, the four headed to Staten Island where they boarded the *Thomas H. Barry*, a troopship converted in 1946 to carry military dependents. Richman spent the trip reading the decisions of the IMT at Nuremberg, while Edith, who spoke fluent German, gave German lessons every morning.

On February 21, 1947, the ship docked at Bremerhaven, Germany, in bitterly cold weather. The next day Richman and his party left by train for Nuremberg where they resided temporarily at the Grand Hotel, pending the assignment of a house. The first night they attended the opera *Carmen* at the Opera House, sitting in Hitler's own box with many of the other American judges. Both Richman and his wife commented in their diaries about the sad state of Nuremberg, Richman noting the "desolation visible" from the hotel windows and Edith marveling "that ½ hours bombing should wreak such terrible destruction."[5]

The Richmans spent the next several days house hunting, sightseeing, visiting the PX where they stocked up on rationed Hershey bars and cigarettes, and getting to know the other judges and their wives, noting in their diaries those who had Purdue or DePauw connections. Richman spent time setting

This was the home of the Richman family while they were living in Nuremberg.

Frank and Edith Richman recorded the effects of World War II bombing raids in photos and in diary entries.

up his office in the Palace of Justice while his family tried to get their bearings in a strange city. Observing the German people on the streets, Edith noted in her diary that "everyone seems to carry some sort of a roomy bag, either a brief case, knap sack, large shopping bag. They tell me that they pick up pieces of wood for fuels."[6] After about a week, the Richmans were assigned a house, two servants, a Chevrolet painted with U.S. Army insignia, and a GI driver. Their living conditions compared to those of a general army officer, and they suffered the shortages of certain foods and other items that affected all of the Americans in Nuremberg.

While waiting for his tribunal to begin, Richman and his wife attended the trial of one of the German doctors who had used inmates of the Buchenwald concentration camp for experiments involving the typhus virus. Both criticized the poor cross-examination by the American prosecutor, Richman noting that "a good Indiana lawyer would not have cross-examined at all and certainly would not have put into his questions his own personal opinions." After hearing the prosecutor's excuse that he had a blinding headache caused by partying the night before, Edith remarked with disdain that "someone ought to tell him why he is over here."[7] They also attended the commencement of the trial of fifteen German justices and heard General Taylor's opening statement.

Both Richmans heard various lectures and talks about Germany and the American military occupation. Edith reported in her diary of one such talk where a speaker told a group of American wives that a responsibility rested upon them to sell democracy to the women of Germany. Another speaker warned the same group of Americans of the possibility of the Germans' indoctrinating them "since they were in the habit of excusing themselves for responsibility for the war and its results."[8] On another day, Edith wrote of a German speaker at an orientation session for American dependents who insulted them for their "luxurious living" and "bad behavior."[9] Clearly Americans in Germany needed to be wary of their presence in a war-torn land and to understand the almost parental-like obligations such presence entailed—to be upright models for American democracy and decency, yet at the same time firm in their commitment to discipline and justice for the perpetrators of war crimes.

At the American Military Tribunal IV, the prosecution filed its indictment against Flick and five of his principal associates on February 8, 1947, and later amended it on March 18, 1947. In his diary for that day, Richman wrote that he had heard Colonel Charles Mays read the amended indictment to Flick, noting that "he was worth $40,000,000, appeared in court in ragged clothes. Awful comedown. . . . Punishment already severe, to come down from his former station in life."[10] Flick, a powerful steel magnate and "probably the richest man in Germany,"[11] headed a steel conglomerate that played a leading role in heavy German industry.

The indictment against Flick and his associates listed five counts: (1) slave labor, based on the forcible deportation of foreign nationals, concentration

Hoosier Justice at Nuremberg

Friedrich Flick, flanked by two guards, appeared before the American Military Tribunal in 1947.

camp inmates, and prisoners of war to work as forced labor in Flick mines and factories; (2) spoliation, based on the seizure of plants and property in France and the Soviet Union; (3) crimes against humanity in the persecution of Jews during the prewar years of 1936–39, specifically the "Aryanization" of Jewish industrial and mining properties; (4) cooperation with the SS (the SS was an elite Nazi paramilitary organization determined by the IMT to be a criminal organization), based on the knowing participation in persecutions and other atrocities perpetrated by the SS and by the giving of large sums of money to the SS; and (5) membership in the SS, based on association with the "Circle of Friends" or "Himmler Circle" that included SS officers and leading industrialists. The *New York Times* reported that the difficulty of gathering records scattered throughout Germany prevented the bringing of an additional charge against Flick of the waging of aggressive warfare. Richman's associates on the bench included Presiding Judge Charles B. Sears, retired Justice of the Court of Appeals of New York, and Judge William C. Christianson, former

The Flick judicial panel (left to right): Frank Richman, Charles Sears (presiding judge), William Christianson, and Richard Dixon (alternate).

Justice of the Supreme Court of Minnesota. Judge Richard D. Dixon of the Superior Court of North Carolina acted as alternate until he left to join another of the tribunals.

A native of the western German region of Westphalia and a self-made millionaire, Flick started in the steel business during World War I and made large profits during the inflationary period that followed. During the Depression of the 1930s, he sold that business to the German government and founded his new empire with the proceeds. Named Flick KG, its interests and holdings included coal and iron ore mines, blast furnaces, smelting, coking and chemical plants, synthetic fuel rolling mills, finished steel products, railroad rolling stock, trucks, airplanes, and various ammunition and armaments. Flick KG controlled all stages of steel production. Its operations extended beyond Germany to include France and the Soviet Union. Claiming to loathe political activity, Flick did not join the Nazi Party until 1937 or 1938, although he had (probably in late 1935) joined the Circle of Friends and through that group contributed funds to the SS. While Flick tried to portray the Circle as a harmless gentlemen's club whose members attended lectures and infrequently visited SS factories, the group's financial contributions helped to finance Heinrich Himmler's pet projects, including deadly experiments on concentration camp inmates.[12] *The New Yorker* described Flick as "the man who helped his friend Herman Göring write the Aryanization statutes and the regulations for the economic exploitation of France and Russia, and who took advantage of the opportunities afforded by his handiwork and by the slave-labor laws to become the wealthiest man in Germany."[13]

From the time of his appointment, Richman, along with many of the other judges, expressed troubling concerns about whether the military courts could properly claim jurisdiction over the defendants. On the ship over to Germany, he read books on international criminal law and found few precedents "of litigated cases in which crimes were defined and the law applied to facts, with final judgment." In writing to Dean Henry B. Witham of the Indiana University School of Law at Indianapolis on May 6, 1947, Sharpnack, Richman's law partner, noted that, "Frank sent me a copy of the indictment, etc., as he did with you, and indicates that he would like to have some legal or spiritual advice on the question of his court having jurisdiction to try Germans for offenses against Germany." In his diary, Richman recounts a judges' conference in Nuremberg in late March 1947 at which the judges debated the jurisdictional issue. He wrote, "We got nowhere on jurisdictional question except to decide that it must be briefed and argued."[14] The next day, he continued, "C[hristianson] & I have done some work on jurisdiction of courts to try for crimes vs. humanity against German nationals. I wish I knew more about international law."[15] On April 9, Richman related that he had discussed with General Taylor "securing authority to show that crimes against humanity were recognized as such by international law prior to 1939," only to learn that Taylor had already requested research on this point. Richman opined that he would like to see "more authority or basic argument" before accepting the conclusion.[16] Ultimately Richman appears to have resolved his inner doubts in favor of jurisdiction. In an article written near the end of his tenure in Nuremberg, he granted that, while there might be some validity to the arguments against jurisdiction, the offenses being tried "are breaches of the law of nations," and cited the U.S. Supreme Court decision in *Milch v. United States* (332 U.S. 789, 68 S.Ct. 92 [1947]). In that case, the Court chose not to intervene in a jurisdictional challenge in a trial of another German industrialist.[17] Richman's basic sense of decency caused him to have similar concerns about the lack of an appeals procedure. He expressed his unease when he wrote:

> In a criminal prosecution in the United States if the trial judge misapplies the law or a jury finds guilt without sufficient evidence, the error may be corrected by a higher court. The Nurnberg tribunals were courts both of first and last resort. The judgment might be reviewed by the Commanding General of the American Zone and the penalties decreased, but otherwise, assuming the court had jurisdiction, the defendants had no remedy, none by appeal and none even by pardon, for these were international courts and their judgments lay beyond the control of the executive of any one of the allied nations.[18]

Despite these reservations, Richman took very seriously his responsibility to assure the fairness of the trial. He felt strongly that the defendants had received just treatment and prided himself on making sure that any errors made were not prejudicial to the defendants. During the trials, he wrote, "Though

Flick defendants in the dock. From left to right: Hermann Terberger, Bernhard Weiss, Konrad Kaletsch, Odilo Burkart, Otto Steinbrink, and Friedrich Flick. The defense counsel is seated in the foreground.

these courts do not believe themselves bound by the constitution or statutes of the United States, nevertheless the judges have applied American fundamental principles of due process in the effort to give every defendant a fair trial."[19]

On April 19, 1947, all of the Flick defendants pleaded not guilty to the charges. Over the course of the next eight months, the tribunal convened 136 times with more than ten thousand pages of evidence introduced. The trial transcript contained 11,026 pages. For the most part, the prosecutors were young, inexperienced American lawyers. Of their lack of trial experience, Richman said, "That was not too great a handicap since the trial was not under the technical procedural rules common to United States courts,"[20] although he noted that the Americans sometimes adopted some of the bad habits of their German counterparts, such as long-windedness. The defendants chose their own German lawyers who were generally very able, some of them having served as counsel to the defendants during the IMT. The United States

Brigadier General Telford Taylor, U.S. chief of counsel, standing at podium, delivers the opening statement in the Flick prosecution.

MAZAL LIBRARY

paid the German lawyers but charged the fees back to Germany as part of the reparations received after the war. Richman described days spent in the courtroom with headphones pressed against the ears of the American judges, causing exhaustion by the end of each week.

On the opening day of the trial, April 19, 1947, General Lucius D. Clay, the U.S. Military Governor, sat at the prosecution table. Taylor, his deputy Thomas E. Ervin, and Charles S. Lyon shared the reading of the 103-page opening statement of charges, which traced the growth of Flick's company and its role in heavy German industry. The prosecution recounted how the defendants had supported Hitler's promises to industry of a stable government, no labor troubles, a rapid rise in production for rearmament, and a new German economic hegemony. In reviewing Flick and his codefendants' close cooperation with the Nazi regime, the prosecution noted their membership in the SS, their contributions of large sums of money to the party, and their aid in the conscription of labor. The opening statement boldly declared that the

Hoosier Justice at Nuremberg

defendants "turned back the clock and revived slavery in Europe," pressuring the Nazi government to obtain slave laborers for their use and employing as many as 40,000 of them at any one time under horrid conditions. Further, it alleged that Flick's concern pushed the German government into dispossessing French and Russian owners of their property, always being careful to legalize its position by getting the government to take possession of the property first before passing it on to Flick.[21]

The procedures used at the trial reflected those employed at the IMT that had been devised by Justice Jackson, chief of counsel at that trial, in collaboration with British, French, and Russian lawyers. These enabled the proceedings to move at a speedy pace. For example, counsel summarized exhibits rather than reading them in full; documents could generally be introduced without extensive preliminary proof; affidavits were readily admitted in cases where witnesses could not be produced in court; and no surprise witnesses were allowed. The judges exhibited impatience with delays and wordiness. In a later speech, Richman noted that "almost any evidence having probative value including hearsay was admitted. The only important test was relevancy." Since there was no jury, the court could disregard any evidence later judged irrelevant. As Richman put it, "the judges were accustomed to sifting the wheat from the chaff ignoring the latter."[22] In general, Richman believed that the relaxed procedures, which he likened to those used before administrative boards, benefited the defendants more than the prosecution.

Called the slave labor count, the first count of the indictment charged the defendants with enslavement and deportation on a large scale of civilians from the countries under German occupation, enslavement of concentration camp inmates, and the use of prisoners of war in war operations. Although Flick KG was initially reluctant to employ forced workers on a large scale, as the war dragged on and the manpower shortage became acute, all of Flick's companies became heavily reliant on such workers. On this count, four of the six defendants received acquittals based in part on the defense of necessity put forth by the German counsel despite vigorous argument by the prosecution that such defense is limited largely to military cases and only allowed in very narrow circumstances. In a later speech, Richman stated his belief:

> Under compulsion of threat and fear of concentration camps or worse, the defendants were compelled to accept the production orders and to take the labor sent by the Nazi Labor Government. There was no substantial evidence of mistreatment.[23]

Flick and his nephew Bernhard Weiss's actions in requesting the government to provide additional laborers in order to run their plants more efficiently deprived them of this defense, and they each received a guilty verdict on the first count.

Richman and the other members of the tribunal have been criticized for misconstruing the doctrine of necessity. The German counsel were actually referring to what might be called the "doctrine of justification," whereby a violation of law is justified when the desired result can be accomplished in no other way. The tribunal, however, construed the doctrine of necessity as one of duress and in its ruling stated:

> This Tribunal might be reproached for seeking vengeance rather than administering justice if it were to declare as unavailable to defendants the defense of necessity here urged in their behalf. This principle has had wide acceptance in American and English courts and is recognized elsewhere.[24]

The judgment stated that the Reich reign of terror created "clear and present danger" for the defendants if they obstructed or hindered the government's plans. Clearly the tribunal focused on the elements of force and fear as the basis for the defendants' actions rather than the justification doctrine.[25] As one commentator put it, "the court's extension of this defense [the doctrine of necessity] to Flick, a corporate officer, seems to have stood precedent on its head."[26] Since the ruling appeared to contradict the earlier ruling on this issue by the IMT, he caustically noted,

> Amazingly, the legal precedent left by this series of trials seems to be that a nineteen-year-old draftee accused of war crimes cannot successfully plead that he was acting under orders, but the owners and directors of multi-billion-dollar companies can.[27]

The second count of the indictment charged all the defendants with spoliation and plunder of occupied territories in violation of the Hague Convention. With weak proof, only Flick was adjudged guilty based on his depriving a French owner of the use of his steel plant during the German occupation of Lorraine. At the trial, the French owner came from England to testify that, after fleeing during the war, he had returned to find his plant in much better condition than when he left.

The third count charged crimes against humanity and took several months to try. The evidence dealt with four separate transactions by which the Flick concern acquired industrial property formerly owned or controlled by Jews. Three of the transactions were outright sales of controlling shares in manufacturing and mining corporations, while the fourth was an expropriation by the Nazi regime of brown coal mines in Germany, from which Flick then acquired the properties. All of the transactions occurred prior to the war. Richman felt strongly from the outset that the court lacked jurisdiction, but his associates wanted to hear the evidence before deciding. Ultimately they all agreed that no jurisdiction existed although in dictum the court found that crimes against property, as opposed to the person, did not rise to the level of crimes against humanity.

The allegations of count four were that Flick and his associate Otto Steinbrinck, knowing of the criminal activities of the SS, contributed funds and influence to its support. Count five charged Steinbrinck with membership in the SS subsequent to September 1, 1939. The IMT had previously declared that membership in the SS was criminal and that knowledge of its criminal activities was generally known throughout the population. To Steinbrinck's assertion that he lacked such knowledge, the tribunal replied:

> But in the face of the declaration of IMT that such knowledge was widespread we cannot believe that a man of Steinbrinck's intelligence and means of acquiring information could have remained wholly ignorant of the character of the SS under the administration of Himmler.[28]

Richman believed that the evidence against Flick and Steinbrinck on count four was weak; both claimed their payments to Himmler had been for cultural purposes. The tribunal seemed to have sympathy for both men but had to follow the mandate of the IMT and held Flick guilty of count four and Steinbrinck of counts four and five. As noted by the *New York Times*, "certain passages in the judgment tended to indicate a degree of compassion for the defendants and a determination to discover all possible mitigating circumstances."[29] The passages cited all seem to indicate that the court simply could not believe that the men could be that evil. In discussing Flick, the judgment noted that he "knew in advance of the plot on Hitler's life in July 1944, and sheltered one of the conspirators." Of Steinbrinck, it said, "It is unthinkable that Steinbrinck, a U-boat commander who risked his life and those of his crew to save survivors of a ship which he had sunk, would willingly be a party to the slaughter of thousands of defenseless persons." The judgment stated that, to both men, membership in the Nazi Party "was a sort of insurance."[30] It accepted their statements that neither believed in the party's ideologies, nor was markedly anti-Jewish, and cited their continued church affiliations as proof of their good character.

In speaking of the trial as a whole, Richman revealed the court's general feeling when he stated, "I think that you will have concluded from this review that these defendants were not guilty of any heinous offenses."[31] In a separate article, Richman distinguished between the harsh sentences imposed by the IMT and what he viewed as the lesser offenses committed by Flick and his associates.

> It was right that war criminals be punished. The German people expected it. But there were different kinds of war crimes and varying degrees of guilt which had to be recognized. The trials would have been subject to condemnation by Germans and Americans alike if all defendants had received long term sentences or the death penalty.[32]

This attitude on the part of Richman and his associates has been criticized, with noted legal historian John Alan Appleman writing:

> [T]he court was apparently unable to feel that offenses by industrialists fell into as severe a category as when committed by a common man [such as an ordinary soldier], particularly when the latter individual actually took the final steps toward the mistreatment or killing of another human being.[33]

Another commentator claimed that the judges in the Flick case were particularly hostile to the prosecution.[34] The verdict on December 22, 1947,

Flick trial in session (Richman is sitting at the top, left).

freed the three defendants found not guilty of any of the charges, while Weiss received a two and one-half years sentence, Steinbrinck, five years, and Flick, seven years. Each got credit for the years spent in jail awaiting trial and judgment. Weiss served about a year, while Steinbrinck died in prison in 1949. Flick unsuccessfully fought his conviction on jurisdictional grounds, going to the District Court of the District of Columbia, the Court of Appeals, and the U.S. Supreme Court, which refused to review his case. By the end of August 1950, Flick was released from prison based on a program in which prisoners were credited with ten days a month for good conduct although many in the United States were highly critical of such early releases due to the nature of the war crimes committed.

Finally, Richman spoke of the reaction of the German people to the trials. He felt sympathy for their resentment of the occupying army that supplied its personnel with good food and gasoline and commandeered the best homes for its officers, at a time when ordinary Germans had little food or fuel. He reported that "many Germans, who had lived under the Nazi regime with their eyes shut and ears closed, were astounded by the revelations of brutality brought forth by the evidence in some of the cases."[35]

In evaluating the ultimate worth of the trials, Richman saw two major benefits. First, he believed that

Hoosier Justice at Nuremberg

the trials were necessary to make good the promises of the allied governments to the world and their warnings to the malefactors, that when came the armistice there would be diligent prosecution in courts of justice of all those in high places responsible for the mass murders, persecutions and other war crimes that were then shocking the sensibilities of all civilized people.[36]

He felt that the country had maintained its self-respect by fulfilling its commitments in this regard. Second, the IMT, the trials in the American, French, and British occupations zones, and in Japan cumulatively made "a very substantial contribution to international criminal law." Richman pointed out that since the Flick trial was the first industrial case, the judges in the Farben and Krupp cases (two of the other industrialists' trials at Nuremberg) later cited on several occasions the opinion of his tribunal as authority. He proudly stated that "I have no doubt that in future war trials the judges will profit by the labor which went into our decisions."[37]

Over the course of the Richmans' yearlong stay in Nuremberg, they seized the opportunity to tour Germany and other parts of Europe. Frequent weekend outings to nearby cities were standard for the American judges and their families. Edith's diary recounted shopping for antiques and local specialties wherever they went, often paying by barter with foodstuffs and cigarettes. Sightseeing, attending cultural events, and taking many long walks filled their time. In addition, Edith described an endless ritual of dinners, cocktail parties, and socializing among all the American jurists and their families. The Indiana group consisted of the Richmans, Curtis Shake, and Clarence F. and Irene Merrell. Merrell was an Indianapolis attorney serving as an alternate judge on the Farben case. The two couples and Shake spent much time together, enjoying what Edith termed "Indiana dinners" in her diary. Daughter Elizabeth was in

BYRON R. LEWIS HISTORICAL COLLECTION LIBRARY, VINCENNES UNIVERSITY

Sightseeing in Germany and other European cities filled the time of the American jurists and their families. The so-called Indiana group (left to right): Edith Richman, Irene Merrell, Clarence Merrell, Frank Richman, Elizabeth Richman, and Curtis Shake pose during an outing.

The Indiana group in Nuremberg (Richman and Shake are on the left in the back row).

great demand among the younger set and never lacked for escorts. The receipt of mail from home was eagerly anticipated and much celebrated.

On September 24, 1947, Edith and Irene set out in a car driven by a young American soldier bound for Augsburg and Munich, with Italy being their ultimate destination. At about five o'clock that afternoon, Richman received word that their car had been involved in a serious accident sometime after leaving Augsburg. The car had apparently skidded on slippery pavement on a temporary bridge, gone through a railing, turned over in the air, and rolled down a twenty-five-foot embankment landing on hard ground. Edith was pinned beneath the car when it landed. Both women sustained significant injuries, and the ambulance initially took them, both unconscious, to a dispensary in Augsburg before then moving them to the 98th General Hospital of the U.S. Occupation forces at Munich. Richman and Merrell immediately left for Munich, about one hundred miles from Nuremberg. When they arrived,

Irene was in the operating room having some cuts sewn up, while Edith was in an oxygen tent with very serious injuries including a fractured skull, pelvis, and ribs. When Richman entered the room, she opened her eyes and said in a weak voice, "I knew you'd come."[38]

Richman recalled the days following Edith's accident as "a nightmare to me" and described her as "sweet, patient, pathetic." She had no memory of anything that had happened after they left Augsburg. The severity of her injuries was borne out by Richman's writing in her diary (which he had undertaken to continue during her illness): "Sent cablegram to Margaret [their daughter] informing fully, so that if she should die the shock to children would not be so great." Richman's devotion to his wife and his despair at her injuries came through when he wrote, "She is a wonderful person. Her innate goodness shows itself in her words when she seems unconscious. During these days she was always thinking of others, never of herself. . . . But the poor little thing is still so frail, her voice so weak, that it is hard to keep the tears away when I stand or sit beside her."[39]

On October 8, 1947, Edith and Irene had improved enough to return home to Nuremberg. Initially in a wheelchair, Edith required the services of a nurse while she slowly regained her strength and health and learned to walk again. When she saw pictures of the accident site for the first time, Edith wrote, "Worse than I could have imagined. I must not forget that I am alive by a miracle and try to give some service to justify it."[40] The process of recovery was long and slow and Edith had to fight to keep her spirits up. By the end of November, as the Flick trial wound down, the Richmans began planning their return to America. Edith reported that Richman worked on part of the judgment on Thanksgiving Day and the days after, writing in her diary, "Frank has been working on his opinion all day, seems to have doubts & difficulties."[41]

Shake and the Merrells threw a farewell party at a restaurant for the Richmans on December 17, 1947, at which Edith noted in her diary the singing of "Back Home Again in Indiana" and, with good humor, wrote that since she was seated between Judges Sears and Shake, she did not have to talk much. The only sour note was her comment that "the German women especially stared at us very contemptuously."[42] Two days later, Edith became ill and required hospitalization for a few days, causing concern that their return to America would be delayed. On December 27, however, they made it out to sea, leaving from Bremerhaven. Two days later, Edith had turned yellow and ended up in the ship's hospital. A diagnosis of hepatitis followed, most likely introduced into her blood stream by plasma she had received after her auto accident.

On the morning of January 6, 1948, the ship docked in New York. Although the army wanted to keep Edith in a nearby hospital, Richman had received permission to take her on the night train to Indianapolis. Transported by ambulance to the train and then met by ambulance in Indianapolis, Edith was taken to the Robert Long Hospital where she eventually recovered, surrounded by her family and friends.

The Richmans felt grateful to be home. Richman recalled that at the end of the Flick case, the army had asked him to stay on as presiding judge in another case about to begin. He turned down the opportunity using the following reasoning:

> It would have been profitable financially for we were able to save a good portion of our compensation, but money is not the only good thing. Before I went I was told we would be through in six months and I made my plans accordingly. The trial dragged to almost a year. I felt that I had done my duty. It was a great experience, enough is enough. We lived comfortably in Nürnberg but there is no place like our Indiana home.[43]

Curtis Shake in front of a bombed structure in Nuremberg.

CHAPTER 4
Shake at Nuremberg

Like his colleague Frank Richman, Curtis Shake arrived in Germany by ship, docking at Bremerhaven and then traveling by train to Nuremberg. It was the late spring of 1947, and Shake learned firsthand within a few days of his arrival of the desperate conditions existing within Germany. He recounted a story that happened on his first day at the Grand Hotel in Nuremberg. Sitting down to a meal in the hotel dining room, he told his young German waiter to bring just a small meal as he was not very hungry. The waiter "almost cried" and begged Shake to order a full meal, explaining that he worked at the hotel primarily to retrieve the remains of his customers' plates. He showed Shake pictures of his two children and stated that "all they get is what I take home."[1] From then on, Shake ordered all that he could at every meal. He also reported seeing starving people behind the hotel sifting through the garbage cans.

On his second day in Nuremberg, Shake decided to walk to the Palace of Justice where the courtrooms were located. He noticed that two young German men were following him and grew concerned for his safety. As he finished a cigarette and tossed the stub in the street, Shake understood suddenly what the men were after as he watched them scour the street to grab the stub. As he put it, "the cigarette was cash." This conclusion was further borne out by the chambermaid at the Grand Hotel who offered to do Shake's laundry for five cigarettes a week. On another occasion he saw an elderly woman picking up used matches from the ground to use to start a fire.

During Shake's stay in Germany, a friend from Terre Haute asked him to check on his wife's cousin who lived near Nuremberg. The friend reported that he had been sending CARE packages to the cousin and wanted to confirm that the German man and his family were truly in need of assistance. While visiting the family, Shake was shocked to observe dried apple peels used as a substitute for tea and knew that the aid being sent was indeed merited. One weekend Shake decided to get away from the hotel and the city, both of which he found depressing. A German friend recommended a hotel in a small village but suggested he take his own groceries with him since there might not be much to eat there. Shake gathered a box of canned meats, canned vegetables, fruit, and other things one could buy at the army commissary. When he arrived at the hotel, he told the proprietor that he would pay him with the food when he checked out but he wanted to eat what the Germans ate while there. He later recalled:

> Well, that night for dinner I had a boiled potato, no seasoning
> in it whatsoever and a little bowl of soup, looked like bouillon, no
> vegetables, no meat in it, just brown water, it was salted and that
> was all I could tell about it. And I had some of this black bread
> that was half bread and half sawdust.[2]

Hoosier Justice at Nuremberg

About a month after his arrival in Nuremberg, Shake took a nostalgic trip to Czechoslovakia, ancestral home of his late wife, Anna Selesky. Anna's father, Alexander Szeleczky, had been born around 1862 near Staré Hory, a mountainous area of the country that had previously been part of Hungary. Staré Hory was a quaint old village of about a thousand people, site of a well-known Catholic shrine, and near several Gypsy villages that put on evening programs of music and dance, one of which Shake attended. In a letter home to his son and daughter-in-law, Shake explained how he had traced his father-in-law's roots. A Catholic priest found a record of Alexander's birth, and a distant cousin showed him where the family had lived. Shake learned that his wife's grandfather had been the keeper of the king's hunting lodge and acted as a guide when the king brought his friends there to hunt deer and wild boar. For that reason, he noted, "Everyone about Staré Hory seemed to regard the Szeleczkys as very important people."[3]

In another village fifteen miles away, Shake located his wife's only living aunt. He walked into her home and, to his great surprise, found pictures on her mantle of himself, his wife, and his son Gilbert, which evoked a strong emotional response in Shake. The aunt was "a very proud and self-sufficient old lady," who told him that she had known of his wife's death but had not written "because she was afraid we would think she was hinting for help."[4] The aunt took Shake to his father-in-law's grave. Alexander had died in 1892 before the rest of his family had immigrated to America.

After he had been in Germany for more than a month, Shake received his official letter of appointment to Tribunal VI of the war crimes court to hear case six, *United States of America vs. Carl Krauch, et al.* (the "Farben case"), which the press viewed as being second only to the International Military Tribunal (IMT) in importance. Shake was named Presiding Judge of Tribunal VI and on November 12, 1947, elected by his peers as Chairman of the Committee of

Farben judicial panel (from left to right): James Morris, Curtis Shake (presiding judge), Paul Hebert, and Clarence Merrell (alternate).

Presiding Judges. I. G. Farbenindustrie A.G. was an enormous chemicals and synthetics combine that played a crucial role in Germany's ability to wage war. The prosecution filed its indictment against twenty-four of Farben's officers and directors on May 3, 1947. One defendant was severed from the case due to ill health so only twenty-three actually stood trial. The indictment had five counts, although not all defendants were charged with each count: (1) planning and waging aggressive war; (2) spoliation; (3) slave labor; (4) membership in the SS; and (5) conspiracy to commit aggressive war. Shake's associates on the bench included Judge James Morris, Justice of the Supreme Court of North Dakota, Paul M. Hebert, Dean of Louisiana State University Law School, and, as alternate, Clarence F. Merrell, a practicing attorney from Indianapolis recommended by Shake.

At the outbreak of World War II, I. G. Farben was the largest chemical combine in the world. Some believed it was the largest corporation of any kind existing at that time. Farben dominated the world chemical business through its vast assets, superior technological know-how, and its formidable array of patents. It held interests in about four hundred business concerns in Germany and five hundred others throughout the world. In addition, it had cartel arrangements with industrial giants, including Standard Oil (New Jersey), DuPont, and Dow Chemical. But Farben was not just a corporate empire. To compensate for Germany's lack of natural resources, Farben produced synthetics of oil, rubber, nitrates, and fibers, thus giving Germany the self-sufficiency it craved. It also manufactured vaccines, sera, and drugs such as aspirin, Novocain, sulfa, and atabrine (for treating malaria), as well as poison gases and rocket fuels. At least four of its scientists earned Nobel Prizes for their work. The twenty-three defendants comprised (with one very elderly exception) all of the living members of the *Vorstand*, or managing board of Farben, plus four subordinates who were intimately associated with such board.

After he received his appointment to the Farben case, Shake confessed later that he "was so ignorant that I thought I. G. Farben was probably the name of a corporation named after Mr. Farben, I. G. Farben."[5] He admitted being surprised when he learned that the defendants included Nobel Prize winners and famed scientists, none of whom were large stockholders of the company nor had any substantial financial interest in Farben other than his individual salary. In contrast to the United States where a man might work his way up the ladder to become the president of a company, in Germany the large companies hired professional executives out of the universities.

Like his colleague Frank Richman, Shake recognized the controversial nature of the Nuremberg trials and questioned their justification. In an interview years later, he noted that U.S. senator Robert A. Taft, a prominent conservative for whom he expressed deep admiration and respect, believed that the trials were wrong. Taft and others thought that the allied powers were applying ex post facto law, i.e., a law that did not exist at the time of the commission of the alleged crime. Shake disagreed with Taft's view, saying:

> But I think there's justification for them on the theory that . . . of a common law of civilization, that it doesn't take a statute or a treaty to make it unlawful to put five or six million people through gas chambers, burn them up, knock their teeth out for the gold fillings, cut the hair of the women and use it to pad mattresses, burn them and take the ashes out for fertilizer on the farms. I think that is just simply against the law of civilization itself. And I've never had any qualms about it, about that.[6]

On another occasion, Shake again defended the tribunals, first mentioning that Germany and other civilized nations had been bound by the Geneva Convention respecting the use of slave labor and military captives. He then likened the basis for the trials to the application of common law in the United States, noting that "murder from time immemorial under American and British jurisprudence has been a common law crime." Shake believed that neither a formal statute nor international law was needed to establish the criminality of killing people in concentration camps. After describing his visits to three such camps and the horrors he had witnessed there, Shake declared, "I've never had any compulsion about the fact that we were applying ex post facto law."[7]

On August 14, 1947, each of the twenty-three defendants in the Farben case pleaded not guilty. The trial began on August 27, 1947, and did not conclude until the middle of June 1948. The trial transcript numbered 15,834 pages. As in the Flick case, many of the German lawyers were veterans of the IMT and all received their pay from the American government. Dressed in long black gowns with velvet collars and long straight shoulder-length hair, the defense attorneys made quite an impression on an observer of the trial writing in *The New Yorker*:

Hoosier Justice at Nuremberg

Farben defendants in the dock (front row) left to right: Carl Krauch, Hermann Schmitz, Georg von Schnitzler, Fritz Gajewski, Heinrich Hoerlein, August von Knieriem, Fritz ter Meer, Christian Schneider, Otto Ambros, Ernst Buergin, and Heinrich Buetefisch; (back row) left to right: Paul Haefliger, Max Ilgner, Friedrich Jaehne, Hans Kuehne, Wilhelm Rudolf Mann, Heinrich Oster, Walter Duerrfeld, Heinrich Gattineau, Eric von der Heyde, and Hans Kugler.

It would seem, as a matter of fact, as if the defense lawyers might overpower the court by sheer numbers. There are more than fifty of them, any one of whom may object to any document, statement, or action of the prosecution, and the objections are so many that in order to get them all registered there is often a queue of bowing, skirted figures waiting at one side of the rostrum. Technically, twenty-three of them, one for each defendant, may cross-examine every prosecution witness. Cross-examination has never been encouraged in German courts, and the defense counsel in Nuremberg have, for the most part, seized upon the practice with joy and admiration.[8]

Years later, Shake reminisced about the German lawyers, saying "they were fine; they were keen. I get letters from some of them yet. I'm very fond of them. . . . They all wore gowns. They were very formal. They'd bow at you all the time when you'd go around."[9]

The prosecution lawyers, "a few young Americans who operate with a minimum of ceremony and no gowns at all," were dedicated to their cause and often wore "desperate expressions."[10] Some Farben sympathizers tried to distract attention from the main issues of the trial by attacking Deputy Chief Counsel Josiah E. DuBois Jr. On the floor of the U.S. House, Representative George Dondero of Michigan made the charge that DuBois was a "known left-winger from the Treasury Department who had been a close student of the Communist Party line."[11] As DuBois soon learned, Dondero's real goal in criticizing him was to blast those prosecuting Farben and to protect Dow Chemical Company, alleged to have aided Farben. In fact, some thought that the case would never come to trial because of "the danger of revelations of connivance on the part of officials of certain American corporations," as *The New Yorker* cynically reported:

> Fat chance (this talk went) that those fellows, with all their influence, would permit any information of such an embarrassing nature to be let loose in court. Among those highly sensitive groups who are inclined to attribute sinister intentions to anyone possessed of either a Buick Roadmaster or a subscription to Fortune, this defeatism was especially oppressive, and members of the prosecuting staff are reported to have experienced some very exasperating moments, during the months they were preparing their cases, in trying to bear up under such remarks as "Hope you aren't working too hard on that Farben business. It'll never be allowed to come to trial, you know."[12]

On the opening day of the trial, General Telford Taylor, chief U.S. prosecutor, and his deputies read the opening statement of charges before a packed courtroom. They made it clear that the case would be based primarily on the knowing participation of the Farben defendants in Nazi plans for conquest long before the war began, and on Farben's extensive use of slaves during the war. The prosecution stated that Farben had been an early leader in the move to bring Adolf Hitler to power in Germany and had complete plans for taking over the chemical industry of each country before Hitler marched into that country. Regarding the use of slave labor, the statement charged that the evidence would prove Farben's extensive use of such labor, including prisoners of war, to build and operate its factories. Further, it continued, Farben had built its own concentration camp in the standard Nazi model to man its synthetic rubber factory adjacent to Auschwitz. About twenty-five thousand of its enforced laborers had died, and those deemed unfit to work at the factory had regularly been sent off to the gas chamber.

Taylor inferred that the Farben officials had not acted out of any genuine patriotic impulses, but rather only to advance Farben interests, and that they had actively participated in Hitler's plans to suit their own ends and achieve their own goals. Taylor correctly divined one of the main defense strategies— to portray the defendants as ordinary businessmen—when he stated:

> The defendants will, no doubt, tell us that they were merely over-zealous, and possibly misguided patriots. We will hear it said that all they planned to do was what any patriotic businessman would have done under similar circumstances. . . . As for the carnage of war and the slaughter of innocents, these were the regrettable deeds of Hitler and the Nazis, to whose dictatorship they, too, were subject.[13]

Taylor firmly rejected this argument, calling the defendants the "master builders of the Wehrmacht." He stated the crux of the prosecution case when he said, "These are the men who made the war possible and they did it because they wanted to conquer."[14] Unfortunately, as will be seen, the judges in part bought into this defense strategy and never could quite view the Farben executives as anything but the businessmen they claimed to be.

The most damning charge in the Farben indictment came in count one. For the first time in history, industrialists faced accusations of planning and waging aggressive war, charges that resembled those heard at the IMT. This count went further than any charge against the Flick defendants. Under this aggressive warfare count, all of the defendants stood accused of allying Farben with Hitler and the Nazi Party; synchronizing Farben's activities with Germany's military planning; participating in and directing preparations of Germany's economic mobilization for war; contributing to the creation of the Nazi military machine for aggressive war; procuring and stockpiling critical war materials; helping to weaken potential enemies (accomplished by entering into cartel arrangements with American companies to prevent shipping of essential war materials to Britain); carrying on propaganda, intelligence, and espionage activities; preparing for and participating in the planning and execution of Nazi aggressions and reaping of spoils from them; and participating in plunder, spoliation, slavery, and mass murder as part of the invasions and wars of aggression. According to count one, Farben's activities contributed to millions of people being murdered, tortured, starved, enslaved, and robbed. Further, "a large part of the world was left in economic and political chaos. . . . The life and happiness of all peoples of the world were adversely affected."[15] Closely related to count one, count five charged the defendants with conspiracy to commit aggressive war.

Count two of the indictment charged the defendants with plunder and spoliation. It claimed that Farben "conceived, initiated, and prepared detailed plans"[16] that would enable it to acquire, with the assistance of the German military, the chemical industries of Austria, Czechoslovakia, Poland, Norway, France, and Russia. Count four alleged membership in the SS by three of the defendants subsequent to September 1, 1939.

The allegations of slavery and mass murder, delineated in count three, formed the crux of the indictment. Without these charges, some believed that "it is doubtful that there would have been any war crimes trial at all."[17] During the war, Farben had attempted to produce a synthetic rubber known as Buna and had found a convenient production site adjacent to the German concentration camp at Auschwitz, Poland. The Farben plant drew upon the plentiful supply of labor found at the camp and disposed of those who became too weak to work by sending them back to the camp. Although the responsibility for disciplining the slave workers lay with the plant manager, it was standard policy to call in the Gestapo to enforce discipline. Subhuman standards of living existed at the plant. Even when evidence mounted of what was really happening in the adjacent concentration camp, the Farben leaders continued construction and operation of the plant, known as Buna Auschwitz, overlooking the evidence and taking no steps to attempt to stop the Nazi atrocities. One commentator noted,

> Of all the alleged and actual crimes of the giant chemical corporation, this proven instance of complicity in the worst deeds of the Nazi regime demonstrated that the practices and objectives of the party and those of the firm, while not identical, nevertheless coincided to a disastrous degree.[18]

Once the trial started, Shake reported that the biggest problem faced was "the matter of procedure." After being in court all day, he complained that the judges had to spend more time at night dealing with procedural problems anticipated to arise the next day. Although they applied the relaxed procedures first employed at the IMT and then used at the Flick trial, new issues continually appeared. For example, Shake reported that the issue of affidavits created "a lot of trouble."[19] While the IMT had authorized the use of affidavits in lieu of witnesses, the Farben tribunal struck any prosecution affidavits from evidence where the witnesses could not be located for cross-examination, counter-affidavits, or interrogatories. Affidavits of deceased persons also were excluded. Two days after the trial began, the *New York Times* reported that the Farben trial had abruptly recessed when a constant stream of defense objections, mainly related to affidavits, had made it impossible to proceed. The *Times* stated that Shake had called the recess "with some show of irritation," and warned the defense lawyers to be prepared to proceed the next day without further delay.[20] The language differences presented another procedural concern for Shake who remembered the problems created in the courtroom:

> We've had as many as four languages being spoken simultaneously in the court room at the same time. Unfortunately, I'm no linguist and the only thing I knew was plain United States. But soon as I got used to wearing about six pounds of metal on my head it was no problem whatever. They were the most expert translation staff that you could imagine. We've had a German lawyer and a French lawyer questioning witnesses, an Italian witness on the stand. Of course, I only hear English. I spoke English. Everything I heard came English. Everything I said, they got in their own language and . . . it worked perfectly.[21]

Hoosier Justice at Nuremberg

As the trial progressed, it became clear that a serious split existed among the judges. General Taylor began the prosecution's case by introducing organizational charts, cartel agreements, patent licenses, correspondence, production schedules, and corporate reports, typical of an antitrust case, not of a war crimes trial. Morris expressed his impatience with this strategy, believing that the documents bore only a slight relation to the required proof in the case. He also failed to see the importance of documents dating back to 1937 that were, as he saw it, "before there were any acts of aggression."[22] Shake appeared to side with Morris on some of these criticisms, believing certain evidence redundant. Hebert dissented from this rebuke of the prosecution, asking the court to keep an open mind toward the evidence. Merrell, the alternate judge, echoed Hebert's plea, stating that he was "sympathetic" to the prosecution's tactics and asking for consideration of evidence if any question existed as to its relevance. In the end, Shake agreed with Morris and blasted his friend Merrell, implying that Merrell's sympathies lay with the prosecution. DuBois recalled that "Shake has been so angry at Merrell that he believed—or wished to suggest he believed—that Merrell was partial to the prosecution staff!"[23]

The defense strategy at the trial had several major thrusts. First, the defense attorneys introduced affidavits detailing efforts of the defendants to protect Jewish employees from the Nazis. Along with this relatively unsuccessful tactic, the defense attempted to show a lack of knowledge by the defendants of what was really occurring in the Buna Auschwitz plant. Again, the overwhelming evidence about the nature of the plant's workers made this claim less than credible. A more effective strategy used by the Farben defendants was the defense of necessity. Witnesses (including Friedrich Flick) testified that German industrialists acted under compulsion from the Nazi regime, claiming that refusal to comply would expose an individual to imprisonment and/or death. Finally, defense counsel likened Farben to similar companies worldwide

MAZAL LIBRARY

Judge Paul Hebert (far right) reads the judgment in the Farben case to defendants in the dock (upper left, under clock).

MAZAL LIBRARY

Brigadier General Telford Taylor (in uniform) and other Farben prosecutors at the reading of the judgment.

including DuPont in the United States and painted the defendants as decent businessmen opposed to communism. This strategy appeared to impress some of the judges, especially Morris.[24]

The announcement of the Farben verdict came on July 29 and 30, 1948, almost a year after the trial began. The divisiveness between the judges continued as Shake denied Hebert's request for additional time to file both a concurrent and a dissenting opinion. Before reading the judgment, Shake referred to the mysterious explosion the previous evening of a high-pressure hydrogenation plant in the French zone of occupation, killing almost two hundred workers. Shake offered condolences to the families and all rose in silent tribute. In the aftermath of the verdict, Shake received criticism for even this small act of decency as showing his partiality for the German people, DuBois claiming that Shake's tone showed "a disproportionate compassion."[25]

After a summary of the charges and supporting evidence that seemed to present a strong case against the defendants, the tribunal went on to acquit all the defendants of counts one and five, the preparation and waging of aggressive warfare and conspiracy. About count one, the court stated,

> The prosecution . . . confronted with the difficulty of establishing knowledge on the part of the defendants, not only of the rearmament of Germany but also that the purpose of rearmament was to wage aggressive war. In this sphere, the evidence degenerates from proof to mere conjecture.[26]

In regard to the conspiracy charge, the court referred to the IMT's caution in this area. It believed that only political leaders with power to control governmental policies could be so charged in the absence of proof of any common knowledge of Hitler's plan.

On count two charging spoliation and plunder, nine of the defendants were found guilty and fourteen acquitted based on the court's finding that inducing an owner to part with his property against his will clearly violated the Hague Convention. All were acquitted on count four, membership in the SS.

On the most important charge of the indictment, count three, the tribunal found five of the defendants guilty, singling out only those who had shared direct responsibility for the construction and operation of the Buna Auschwitz plant. The defendants had claimed the defense of necessity in regard to their use of slave labor, arguing that they had no choice but to comply with Nazi dictates. The court asserted that such defense was only available if one had no moral choice as to his course of action:

> It follows that the defense of necessity is not available where the party
> seeking to invoke it was, himself, responsible for the existence or
> execution of such order or decree, or where his participation
> went beyond the requirements thereof, or was the result of his
> own initiative.[27]

While the court did not believe that Farben had deliberately pursued an inhumane policy with regard to the workers, nonetheless, the evidence proved that the Buna Auschwitz plant was a private project and that the five defendants had taken the initiative in procuring slave labor and had at least partial responsibility for the workers' mistreatment. The court stated:

> We are convinced beyond a reasonable doubt that the officials in
> charge of Farben construction went beyond the necessity created by
> the pressure of governmental officials and may be justly charged with
> taking the initiative in planning for and availing themselves of the use
> of concentration camp labor.[28]

In the end, the tribunal acquitted ten defendants on all counts. The remaining thirteen received relatively light prison sentences, ranging from two to eight years. Almost five months later, Hebert filed a dissenting opinion with respect to count three covering the use of slave labor. Contending that the defense of necessity was not sustained, Hebert believed that the evidence justified a finding of guilt for all of the defendants other than the three who were not members of Farben's board of directors. Merrell, who did not have a vote, reportedly sided with Hebert in this matter, both maintaining that the majority had ignored many facts in its findings.

The prosecution and others reacted to the judgment with shock and outrage. Writing in *The Nation*, Howard Watson Ambruster called the ruling "appalling" and declared that "the court has failed in its duty to render justice, strengthen international law, and destroy the seeds of future wars."[29] Within four years, DuBois wrote a book containing a passionate account of the trial in which he stated, "The sentences were light enough to please a chicken thief, or a driver who had irresponsibly run down a pedestrian."[30] In his retelling, DuBois revealed Merrell's "obvious disgust" at the judgment and his own occasional feelings of antipathy toward Shake and Morris, particularly the later. He recounted the journey home from Germany on the *General Patrick*, a former army transport, along with Hebert, Merrell, and Morris. The split between the judges became even more apparent when Hebert and Merrell invited DuBois to eat at their table every day, a table that did not include Morris. During the course of the trip, Hebert revealed to DuBois that by the end of the trial, he believed that the indictment had been proven many times over. Convinced that the verdict would have been much different had Hebert and Merrell sat as a majority on the court, DuBois's intense feelings about the Farben trial plagued him for years and led him to question what had caused Shake and Morris to find the way they had:

I still feel the same stifling anger today that I felt many times during and since that trip. I was reliably informed that, even before the trial started, one of the judges had expressed the view that he didn't believe it was ever intended that industrialists be brought to account for preparing and waging an aggressive war. Surely something stronger than such preconceived notions had distorted the facts in their minds. But what?[31]

In the years since the Farben trial, commentators have analyzed the judgment and tried to understand why the punishment seemed so mild compared to the gravity of the offenses. In his book-length study of the Farben company, Joseph Borkin implies that some of the judges' remarks and attitudes reflected "the prevailing atmosphere of the cold war."[32] DuBois concluded that Shake and Morris ruled on the basis of fear, "their own great fear of the trend of events in 1948."[33] Others who have echoed this sentiment include Robert E. Conot who wrote:

> Three judges were brought to Nuremberg from the United States for each trial, and their judgments tended to reflect the tide of events. The menace presented by the Soviet Union blurred the inhumanities of the Nazi era. The McCarthyite chorus attributed the trials to a Communist plot.[34]

Raymond Stokes, another observer who wrote about Farben during the years after World War II, doubts Borkin's premise and offers two reasons for the weak sentences. First, he claims, "the mild punishments fit with the American judicial tradition of light sentences for 'white-collar' crimes." Second, Borkin strongly believed that the prosecution put on a poor case and cites as an example the prosecution strategy of beginning its case not with the horrors of Auschwitz

Hoosier Justice at Nuremberg

but instead with organizational charts of the huge Farben empire, a strategy more suited to an antitrust rather than a criminal case.[35]

As the relationship between the United States and the Soviet Union worsened in the years after the war ended, interest among the American public in war crimes declined. By the end of 1950, almost all of the Farben and Flick defendants remaining behind bars had been released or were scheduled for release in the near future. On January 31, 1951, John J. McCloy, U.S. High Commissioner for Germany, announced a mass sentence commutation for German war criminals that served to ensure equity in sentencing and rectify procedural inconsistencies among the various trials and to establish good relations with the new West German government.[36]

Did Shake show partiality to the Farben defendants as DuBois implies in his book? Does that explain his vote to acquit many of the defendants and impose only light sentences on the rest? The claim that Shake had a bias in favor of Germans and Germany received considerable attention in the months following the verdict. *Prevent World War III*, a magazine dedicated to making sure that Germany would pay for its war crimes, published a virulent article impugning Morris's wife for befriending Lilly von Schnitzler, wife of one of the Farben defendants, and Shake for his cordial relations with the German counsel:

> Still another amazing incident occurred in Nuremberg, one concerning Judge Curtis G. Shake, who presided at the Farben trials. This judge had the brilliant idea of inviting German defense attorneys to dinner at the Grand Hotel, where Germans were generally denied the right of admittance.
>
> Apparently Judge Shake was greatly impressed by his talks with the German lawyers as he let no occasion slip without pointing out what nice and brilliant people the Germans were. It is said that he

went to Germany armed with the conviction that the trial of German industrialists was never contemplated by the Charter (Law No. 10) under which he was operating, and this despite the fact that under this particular law it was mandatory to consider guilty all persons who have committed those acts and crimes defined in the Charter.

Incidentally, Judge Shake's picture has been prominently displayed in German newspapers after the Farben verdict. Significantly enough, the weekly "Christ und Welt" of Stuttgart, featured the picture with the following caption:

"The President of the U. S. Military Tribunal in the Nuremberg I. G. Farben trial, who excelled by his just conduct of the proceedings, by his absolute objectivity and disregard for all vindictive sentiments, as well as by his endeavor to understand the nature of German conditions between 1933 and 1945."

Maybe these occurrences have no significance. Perhaps nothing sinister should be derived from them. But they may shed some light on the reasons for the shocking leniency shown the Farben criminals.

Maybe our readers know why the I. G. Farben criminals deserved so much understanding and leniency? We don't.[37]

Drew Pearson, author of the nationally syndicated "Washington Merry-Go-Round" column, wasted no time in repeating the allegations made in *Prevent World War III* in a column that ran in November 1948. Using almost identical language under the heading "Nuremberg's Social Season," Pearson wrote:

Some interesting things have been taking place at Nuremberg, where high-placed German war criminals are supposed to be on trial for their lives, not enjoying the winter social season. . . . Another jurist, Judge Curtis G. Shake of Knox County, Indiana, conceived the brilliant idea of inviting several German defense attorneys to dinner at the Grand Hotel, where Germans generally are denied admittance.

Judge Shake presided at the trial of the I. G. Farben industrialists, who operated one of Hitler's chief war industries and who also conducted one of the most atrocious slave-labor camps. It's significant that the I. G. Farben defendants got off with lenient sentences.[38]

Shake, who by that time was back in Indiana, read Pearson's column in the *Indianapolis Star* and reacted immediately. In a letter to Pearson dated November 12, 1948, largely reprinted in the next day's *Star*, Shake vehemently denied the allegations and demanded a full public retraction:

> This is to advise you that there is not the slightest semblance of truth in your statement, and I should like very much to know the source of your misinformation. I never invited any German lawyer to the Grand Hotel, or any other place—never had any thought of doing so—and never fraternized with any of them socially, or otherwise, at any time or place during my service in Nurnberg or since. My only associations with these men were in the court room or in my office and these contacts were conducted strictly on a professional basis, with due regard, always, for the proper relationship that should exist between trial judges and attorneys practicing before them. I defy you or anyone else to successfully challenge my statements.[39]

Shake went on to say that while he had no argument with anyone who chose to criticize the judgment, he disagreed with those who questioned the integrity of the members of the court. Further, he disavowed those who believed in the guilt of all the defendants before the trial had even begun, saying that the tribunal had worked hard to apply international law in a just manner, resisting vengeance and the urge to apply "vindictive justice upon a defeated people."[40] Pearson responded to Shake acknowledging that his information had been inaccurate and expressing his regret. That appeared to be the end of the incident until out of nowhere, the allegations reappeared eleven years later.

In his criticism of the judgment, DuBois had especially noted the case of Max Ilgner, one of the Farben defendants receiving lenient treatment from Shake and Morris. Despite being sentenced to three years in prison for plundering, he was given credit for time served and released immediately after the judgment. Ilgner apparently remained on good terms with Shake; DuBois reported that Ilgner wrote to Shake a few months later informing him that he was about to enter a religious order. On November 10, 1948, Shake replied to Ilgner, offering to recommend him to British Major General Sir Alec Bishop, the Military Governor at Dusseldorf. In his book, DuBois included without comment Shake's entire letter to Bishop in which Shake called Ilgner "a man of fine intellect and capacity" and his conviction, an "unfortunate and tragic experience."[41]

On January 14, 1960, Shake received a confidential tip from a friend in the newspaper business alerting him that Pearson's column scheduled for publication on January 16 would repeat the old allegations about Shake inviting Farben's German attorneys to dinner at the Grand Hotel as part of a story about the resurgence of anti-Semitism in Europe. Shake immediately sent a telegram to Pearson reminding him of the prior events and warning that if publication ensued, he would hold Pearson accountable. Pearson claimed to have telegrammed instructions to newspapers around the county to kill that portion of his column. However, his directive apparently failed to reach at least one of its targets, as the column, including the portion on Shake, ran as scheduled in the *Chicago American*.

Correspondence ensued between Shake and Pearson as Shake announced his intention to take appropriate steps for redress:

Hoosier Justice at Nuremberg

This is a most serious charge to make against one who has spent a life-time in establishing and maintaining a good reputation for professional probity, and I do not propose to let the matter pass unnoticed. The republication of this charge with knowledge of its falsity and a warning not to do so, is wholly inexcusable and is nothing less than a deliberate and malicious libel on your part.[42]

While taking full responsibility for the error, Pearson's response to Shake in a letter dated February 1, 1960, reflects a far from conciliatory attitude. Pearson noted that in 1948, when the matter had first come up, he had addressed certain questions to Shake that Shake had never answered. These questions related to Shake's letter to Bishop regarding Ilgner, Shake's alleged preconceived notion that industrialists should never have been brought to trial, Shake's alleged bias toward the defense in the Farben case, and certain portions of the judgment's majority opinion that exonerated Farben. Unfortunately, the surviving records do not indicate what actions if any Shake took after receiving Pearson's letter, and Shake never mentioned Pearson in any of his correspondence or speeches about his experiences at Nuremberg. Most likely, the matter ended with the exchange of letters.

In the waning months of the trial, Shake made plans to visit a few places in Europe before returning to Indiana. In May 1948 he wrote an Indiana friend of his plans and revealed his weariness when he concluded, "This has been a unique experience for me but I've had enough and, as I feel now, I don't care whether I ever go anywhere again."[43] After announcing the judgment, Shake accepted an offer to visit Paris from one of the French judges presiding at the French military tribunals. The Frenchman showed his delight at Shake's visit by closing his office and acting as his guide for a few days. Being as he hailed

BYRON R. LEWIS HISTORICAL COLLECTION LIBRARY, VINCENNES UNIVERSITY

Shake and his escort visit a concentration camp.

BYRON R. LEWIS HISTORICAL COLLECTION LIBRARY, VINCENNES UNIVERSITY

BYRON R. LEWIS HISTORICAL COLLECTION LIBRARY, VINCENNES UNIVERSITY

Shake toured many places during his yearlong stay in Europe. This photo was taken in Garmisch in 1947.

This photo of Shake in Nuremberg shows the damage done by Allied bombs.

from Vincennes, Indiana, Shake had mentioned his desire to visit Vincennes, France, so a trip was arranged. Shake recounted that about halfway there, six motorcycles appeared to escort his car and lead it into the city of Vincennes. Confused about what was happening, Shake later told of his embarrassment at being honored during his visit:

> It didn't dawn on me until I wandered around past the castle and
> so forth and got to the city hall and stopped. By golly, there was a
> reception committee. I hadn't shaved that morning to tell you the
> truth. My shirt was not too good. . . . Here came his honor and the
> council, big red ribbon across with medals all up and down his coat.
> So I grabbed my coat and got out and slipped it on and I got out of
> the car and felt like a fool. And he came up and bowed and kissed
> me on the cheek and reached in and pulled out a roll and untied that
> red, white and blue ribbon . . . I thought where am I going to end up
> on this thing, about the friendship and the fraternal spirit between
> Vincennes, France, and the United States and the two citizens of
> the great cities meeting and so forth. I just had to ad lib. I felt like a
> doggone fool.[44]

Upon his return to Indiana, Shake spoke at the Indiana Historical Society in Indianapolis about his experiences in Germany. He maintained that the United States needed to be prepared to stay in Germany for a generation to prevent a third world war. He saw the education of German children as the best way for America to ensure that "another race of Nazis does not arise out of the havoc."[45] In speeches and articles, Shake expressed his belief that the United States owed the German orphans "food, education, and liberty."[46]

For years after his return from Nuremberg, Shake received letters and on occasion visits from Germans, among them Farben defendants and their families and others who had been involved with the trials and wanted to thank him for his benevolence and thoughtfulness. One of his more frequent correspondents was Lilly von Schnitzler, the same person whose friendship with Mrs. Morris had caused rumors to circulate in Nuremberg. Despite all that had happened, both Lilly and her husband remained grateful to Shake for his "kind and understanding feelings during the years of hardship in Germany." Lilly brought up the matter of clemency for the Farben defendants in her correspondence with Shake, and he responded to her enquiries in a letter of March 27, 1950:

> My views with respect to the defendants in the Farben case being proper subjects for the executive clemency have already been expressed, and I trust that before too long the cases of each of them will be reviewed and considered. The offenses for which they were convicted are clearly distinguishable from many of the others who were found guilty at Nurnberg.[47]

In mid-1949, Ernst Achenbach and his wife traveled to Vincennes to visit with Shake in his home and enjoy his hospitality. During the war, Achenbach had been chief of the political section of the German embassy in Paris. Afterwards, he became a leading corporate attorney and a prominent defense attorney for accused former Nazi officials (including one of the Farben defendants).[48] One of the purposes of Achenbach's trip to the United States and a matter that he discussed with Shake was the possible release on parole of the German industrialists still incarcerated for war crimes. Achenbach went on to Washington, D.C., where he met with Ambassador Robert D. Murphy at the State Department to address the same issue. In a letter to Murphy dated September 14, 1949, Achenbach wrote:

Judge Shake authorized me to state as his opinion that given the fact that practically all of the defendants in the Farben Trial still remaining in prison had served more than half of their sentences he thought that releases on parole were warranted since, as he expressed it, none of the defendants had any part in atrocities nor could one speak in their cases of moral turpitude . . . Judge Shake added expressly that he would be glad to give this opinion in writing.[49]

Sentiments such as these along with those expressed in the letter to von Schnitzler quoted above do nothing to dispel the belief that Shake harbored undue sympathies for the Farben defendants. While many would argue with his belief that enslaving workers against their will does not involve moral depravity, no one would deny that Shake was an extremely compassionate person, concerned about the welfare of even the vanquished.

When the trial ended, tension between the judges clearly existed. However, as the years passed, Shake maintained his cordial relationship with all of the others and held no grudge against anyone. In writing his book, DuBois sent the manuscript to Hebert and Merrell for comments and gave them credit for their suggestions in the book's acknowledgments. Shake knew nothing of the book until Merrell innocently asked him if DuBois had also contacted him. Even knowing that DuBois had bypassed him in asking for commentary on his manuscript, Shake promptly wrote to DuBois and very cordially expressed his interest in the project and his "keen anticipation" for the finished product. DuBois's response was equally cordial, concluding with these words:

I have told this story basically as I see it realizing, of course, that others probably saw it differently. I was guided constantly by my conviction that unless I was completely honest in relating the facts as

I saw then, I would be rendering a disservice to the cause and shirking my responsibility.[50]

In 1961 the film *Judgment at Nuremberg* premiered in theaters around the country. Written by Abby Mann, the movie is a fictionalized account of one of the Subsequent Proceedings, the trial of the German judges who carried out the laws promulgated by the Nazi state. While no official publication credits Shake as being the inspiration for the character of the presiding judge in the movie, portrayed by Spencer Tracy, many in his hometown of Vincennes claim to know this as fact. In a letter to Morris dated January 20, 1961, Shake writes of being contacted by Mann, and spending several evenings with him in New York "discussing the philosophy of the Nuremberg Trials." Shake believed that Mann appreciated his input, saying: "He was noncommittal as to his approach, but I believe I had some influence in giving him the proper point of view."[51] A local Vincennes newspaper reported, "Curtis G. Shake is going to be in the movies—figuratively." In addition to noting his meeting with Mann, it claimed that Hollywood was reproducing Shake's Nuremberg courtroom for the film. Mann promised Shake an invitation to the premiere showing of the movie.[52] Tracy's character in the film bears some resemblances to Shake—he arrives in Germany alone as a widower from a small town (in Maine, not Indiana). At the end of the movie, perhaps to acknowledge Shake's contribution, Tracy's aide asks him if he has heard that the verdict in the Farben case has just been announced. Also, one of Tracy's colleagues on the bench is named Curt, possibly another way of recognizing Shake's input. Regardless, Shake no doubt enjoyed every minute of his notoriety in the local press.

At the end of his time in Nuremberg, Shake decided that he would refrain from revealing his true feelings regarding the tribunals until fifteen or twenty years had passed, allowing the distance of time to give him some

Hoosier Justice at Nuremberg

perspective. He kept that vow until the late 1960s when he finally began to express the concerns that he had felt at the time and continued to feel. While Shake accepted the legitimacy of the tribunals, he questioned their makeup, objecting mainly to their American nature: "We were an American tribunal. . . . We were appointed by the President of the United States. We represented the victor. The defendants were citizens of the loser of the war." Shake believed that an impartial tribunal from neutral countries would have been preferable since the judges then would be neutrals and not "the victor trying the vanquished."[53] Pointing to the International Court of Justice at The Hague (Netherlands) as an example of how such a court might be organized, Shake acknowledged that such court only had jurisdiction when both parties agreed to submit the controversy to it. Thus, the International Court was not the answer, only a step in the right direction toward a true system of international law that he believed would come in time. Shake reflected:

> The Bar Association is always talking about a world of law, not of force. I think in due time . . . I'm hopeful enough to think that the civilized nations of the world will agree on a code of conduct in time of war and set up the skeleton of a tribunal that will try it and get away from the charge that the tribunal is [powerless] to try that.[54]

Shake foresaw a court that would take a strong position on "crimes against civilization." Despite these reservations, he believed that all of the American judges in Nuremberg had done everything possible to give the defendants fair and impartial trials, knowing that the same rules applied there might someday be used against Americans "if we should have the misfortune to lose a war."[55]

Richman and Shake in Germany, with driver, 1947.

CHAPTER 5
Back Home in Indiana

After his return to Indiana in early 1948, Frank Richman resumed his teaching career at the Indiana University School of Law, teaching classes at both the Bloomington and Indianapolis campuses. The university named him professor emeritus after he retired in 1952. Richman remained active in the legal community, serving as an arbitrator in several labor disputes and as a special judge in Indiana circuit courts. In November 1952 at a meeting of the law alumni, Julian Sharpnack, Richman's former law partner, presented to the law school a portrait of Richman painted by Randolph Coats. Attorneys, alumni, faculty, students, and friends contributed the funds for the painting. Sharpnack spoke of his friend's teaching career:

> He had no doubt been an efficient teacher and his known industry
> and desire to be exactly right, in an effort to help, may at times cause

RICHMAN FAMILY

students to feel that he was too exacting. If there be any such, let me assure them from personal experience that there reposes beneath that apparent gruff veneer a most kindly heart. Frank's student attitude is summed up in a story to me by a graduate of not too many years, who stated, that the only trouble between him and Judge Richman in law school was, that he didn't have sense enough to know that Judge Richman was trying to make a lawyer out of him.[1]

Unfortunately, Richman's retirement ended after only four years with his death on April 28, 1956. He had been ill for about six months and died at his home in Indianapolis at the age of seventy-four. The funeral and burial took place in Columbus, Indiana, with Curtis Shake taking his place as one of the honorary pallbearers. Among the many eulogies written, the Bartholomew County Bar Association passed a resolution that began: "The lives of great Americans are written in services—services to their communities, to their states, to their nation, and in all to their fellow men. Judge Frank N. Richman measured high in all these categories."[2]

Richman's friend and fellow Rotarian, Yandell C. Cline, speaking before the Columbus Rotary Club, recounted Richman's courage when faced with political pressure:

> I feel that here I should relate to you a story I've heard many times. I cannot prove it but I've heard it so often I believe it to be true. Frank Richman was defeated for re-nomination to the Supreme Court because of his high standard of legal ethics. He refused to "bend the law a little" for political purposes. And, the politicians saw to it that he was not renominated.
>
> As I said earlier, I cannot prove that this story is true. I do know that Frank Richman had courage—that he had an

Hoosier Justice at Nuremberg

almost religious devotion to the law. I do know that he could not compromise with principle. Faced with a decision between "good politics" and "good law," Frank Richman would take but one course—the right one.[3]

Reflecting the rich diversity of Richman's life, the faculty of Indiana University passed a resolution in his memory which ended as follows:

He loved his family, his church, his profession, his home town, a game of bridge, a fishing trip, and traveling. Death interrupted his travels after retirement from teaching. He was 74 years old. But age, in this case, is of minor importance. As a participant in living, his span was about three lifetimes.[4]

Unlike Richman, Curtis Shake lived almost thirty years after his return from Nuremberg. He continued to practice law and remained dedicated to his beloved Vincennes community until the end. Going back there in 1949, he immediately became involved in a campaign to develop Vincennes University as a living memorial to William Henry Harrison by moving the campus to Harrison Park. He also served as president of the Vincennes Chamber of Commerce. That same year, Indiana Governor Henry Schricker named him Chairman of the Indiana Territory Sesquicentennial Commission. He found personal happiness again by wedding Alice Killion Hubbard on January 2, 1952. Together, they had one child, Susan, born December 27, 1952. Gilbert, Shake's son from his first marriage, died in 1968, followed two years later by Alice Shake's death in June 1970.

In 1957 Shake served as a member of the Indiana Lincoln Sesquicentennial Commission and, two years later, represented the State of Indiana on a Lincoln Year tour of Japan. Since 1923 he had served on the Vincennes University

Board of Trustees, serving at times as secretary, vice president, president, and chairman. He finally decided the time had come to resign as its president in 1966, although he remained board president emeritus. Shake could not stay idle for long though, agreeing in 1971 to fill a vacant Knox County Council seat. Professionally, Shake kept busy with his law practice from which he did not retire until age eighty-eight and by his continued involvement with federal mediation boards. President Harry Truman appointed him to a fact-finding board in 1949 to help settle a strike crippling the Wabash Railroad. In 1960 President Dwight Eisenhower named him to a three-member emergency board to stave off a strike threatened by the Brotherhood of Railroad Trainmen against the Long Island Railroad.

Throughout his life, Shake continued his association with the Gimbel family. When Gimbel Brothers stores celebrated its one hundredth anniversary in Vincennes in 1942, he served as the toastmaster. He would occasionally visit with Bernard Gimbel (Jacob Gimbel's nephew) and his wife in their Greenwich, Connecticut, home. Prior to leaving for Nuremberg, Gimbel presented Shake with a going-away present—a bottle of champagne that he had received as a gift from Eddie Rickenbacker, the flying ace of World War I.

Shake's interest in history inspired him to write several publications dealing with Vincennes's story, including *Vincennes University: A Brief History, 1801– 1951* (1951) and *Vincennes: The Old Post on the Wabash: Its Place in American History* (1965). For more than forty years, he pursued with passion the collecting of signatures of every president of the United States from George Washington to Richard Nixon, a collection that he donated to the Vincennes Historical and Antiquarian Society in 1973. Shake explained that it had all begun with a personal letter to him from Herbert Hoover in 1930 in which Hoover had commended him for his work on Vincennes's celebration of the one hundredth anniversary of the migration of Abraham Lincoln's family from Indiana to Illinois. When asked what had led him to amass his collection, Shake said in his folksy manner, "I just got started on it and couldn't quit. It's like holding a bear's tail, I couldn't let loose."[5] In addition to Hoover, Shake also received personal correspondence from Presidents Franklin Roosevelt, Truman, and Eisenhower. He obtained the rest of the signatures by a combination of trading and purchasing: "They've been given to me, peddled to me, found in second-hand and antique shops, and friends have helped me out a lot."[6] The collection includes personal notes, administrative forms, land purchase agreements, and letters of appointment.

Throughout his later years, Shake received numerous honors in recognition of his lifetime of service. In 1975 he was selected for membership in the prestigious Indiana Academy, an organization established by the Associated Colleges of Indiana to honor persons with Hoosier backgrounds whose accomplishments have brought national recognition to themselves and the state. The following year, the Indiana Commission of the Aging and Aged named him the Indiana Senior Citizen of the Year. In his acceptance speech, Shake urged the audience to "get busy. You can't ever stop doing things for your fellow man."[7]

On September 11, 1978, Shake's long and productive life came to an end at the age of ninety-one. The funeral and burial took place in Vincennes. While the many obituaries written about him lauded Shake's service on the Indiana Supreme Court, as a judge at Nuremberg, and his role in building Vincennes University, what they also recalled was his wisdom, wit, and warmth. One editorial recalled:

> But what most of us who knew Curt Shake will really remember
> about him is how he would share his wisdom and memory. He was a

story teller who could make an incident in early Vincennes history or in his courtroom experience live.[8]

Another observer noted that, "We used to say, you could wake Judge Shake up from a deep sleep, stand him on his feet and he could make a speech."[9] A friend wrote of him:

> As anyone who knew him well knows, he was an entertaining conversationalist whose stories came from a bottomless well. . . . But the judge's great contribution to his community came from his vision of what could be and his prodding of others to keep his vision alive.[10]

The *Indianapolis Star* recognized Shake by recounting his service to the state, the nation, and Vincennes University and concluded,

> His death this week at the age of 91 ended a life recognized with many honors, a life in which he never ceased seeking useful things to do.[11]

Shake returned from Germany to Vincennes where he practiced law and remained active in community affairs.

After his service at Nuremberg, Richman resumed his teaching career at the Indiana University School of Law.

BYRON R. LEWIS HISTORICAL COLLECTION LIBRARY, VINCENNES UNIVERSITY

RICHMAN FAMILY

CONCLUSION

This book has attempted to highlight the unique contributions of two Hoosiers to one of the defining events of the twentieth century—World War II and its aftermath. After distinguished legal and judicial careers within Indiana, each stepped onto the world stage with his participation in the Nuremberg tribunals. Despite lingering doubts about the legitimacy of American judges having jurisdiction over German nationals, Frank Richman and Curtis Shake both supported the notion that the crimes committed by the German industrialists in supporting and enabling Adolf Hitler's regime breached all standards of civilized society and could truly be deemed crimes against humanity. After listening to months of testimony and reviewing scores of documents, both joined judges from around the country in holding individual German businessmen liable for their actions in using forced labor in their factories and in seizing property from private owners in occupied countries.

Richman and Shake treated the defendants in the Flick and Farben tribunals with respect, impartiality, and in accordance with American standards of fairness. In doing so, they brought honor and pride to their home state and country. This book serves as a testament to their contributions and to educate a new generation of Hoosiers about the role these leading citizens of Indiana played in events that, more than sixty years later, still resonate across the world.

APPENDIX
Erin Gobel

Frank Richman and Curtis Shake were not the only Hoosiers to participate in the Nuremberg Trials. At least four lawyers with Indiana connections, Arthur Donovan, Frederick Baer, F. Jay Nimtz and Edwin K. Steers served at Nuremberg.

Arthur Donovan was born in New York City in 1910 and grew up near Boston, Massachusetts. He earned his law degree from American University in 1937 and worked briefly for the National Recovery Administration. In 1938 Donovan accepted a position at the new National Labor Relations Board. The next year he became a regional attorney for the NLRB in Indianapolis. After Donovan was drafted into the Army Corps in 1942, he was sent to Atlanta, Georgia, to handle negotiations with defense contractors.

When World War II ended, Donovan was sent to Nuremberg "because of his reputation in the military for vigorous representation in labor disputes."[1] During the trials, Donovan took depositions from witnesses and defendants. Donovan helped prosecute General Anton Dostler, who became the first German general to be executed for war crimes. He also honored Dostler's last request by delivering a letter and personal effects to Dostler's family. In 1946 Donovan joined the Evansville, Indiana, law firm of Kahn, Dees, Donovan & Kahn as a labor law expert. He often worked in volatile labor situations and was once struck in the ear with a baseball bat while trying to help foremen cross a picket line.[2] He often spoke of his experiences at Nuremberg to local school students. Donovan retired in 1992 and died in 2000 at the age of eighty-nine.

Frederick Baer was born in Frankfurt, Germany, in 1910. The Baer family moved to South Bend, Indiana, sometime before Baer reached college age. He attended Notre Dame School of Law, graduating in the 1930s, and began practicing law in 1936 in South Bend.

After World War II ended, former South Bend mayor and powerful lawyer Eli Seebirt suggested that Baer apply for the U.S. prosecution team at Nuremberg, and Baer left for Germany in 1946. Baer thought this position was his "chance to contribute to the war effort, since he was too old . . . to serve during the war."[3] Baer prosecuted low-ranking Nazis, including guards and camp commanders. He also worked on the team that prosecuted the makers of Zyklon B gas, a cyanide-based gas often used in Nazi gas chambers. In 1947 Baer returned home to his South Bend law practice. He served on a redevelopment commission for ten years, invested money in Broadway plays, and served as a consultant and buyer for Notre Dame's Snite Museum of Art. Baer died in 2001.

F. Jay Nimtz was born in South Bend, Indiana, in 1915. He earned a bachelor's degree in 1938 and a law degree in 1940, both from Indiana University. Nimtz was drafted into the army in 1941, serving as a criminal investigator during the war. Remaining in Europe, Nimtz served as the assistant executive officer to Supreme Court Justice Robert Jackson at

Nuremberg. Photographs and contemporary accounts indicate Nimtz as an intimate member of Jackson's team. These lawyers, from both the public and private bar, collaborated closely with lawyers from Russia, France, and England to collect evidence from German records.[4] Nimtz was discharged in 1946, after earning medals from seven different countries.

After unsuccessful runs for public office (South Bend city judge and Saint Joseph County prosecutor), Nimtz was elected to the Eighty-fifth Congress (1957–59) as a Republican Representative from the Third District of Indiana. While in Congress, Nimtz introduced a successful bill to celebrate the 150th anniversary of Abraham Lincoln's birth and was then appointed to the Lincoln Sesquicentennial Commission by the House. Nimtz's re-election campaign was unsuccessful, and he returned to South Bend to practice law. He served on the South Bend Redevelopment Commission, the Indiana Air Pollution Control Board, and the Indiana Environmental Management Board. A local public service award is named in his honor. Nimtz died in South Bend in 1990.

Edwin K. Steers, born in Indianapolis in 1915, was part of a pioneer family from Orange County. He earned a bachelor's degree in 1935 and a law degree in 1937, both from Indiana University. He joined his father, a prominent member of the Indiana Republican Party, at the firm Steers, Klee, Jay and Sullivan. During the 1940s, Steers served as a prosecutor for Marion County. Steers joined the Navy in 1943, serving on a PT boat in Europe and participating in the Normandy invasion.[5] Following the war, Steers helped to prosecute camp guards at the Belsen-Bergen concentration camp in Luneburg, Germany, and worked under Justice Robert Jackson preparing cases at Nuremberg against high-ranking Nazi officials.[6]

Returning from Europe, Steers briefly resumed his position with the Marion County prosecutor's office before being recalled to active duty during the Korean War. In 1952, while overseas, he was elected as Indiana's attorney general. He served three terms leaving office in January 1965. Frequently mentioned as a candidate for lieutenant governor and governor, Steers never ran for either post.[7] Instead, he returned to private practice. He was an active member of the American Legion, the Marion County Republican Veterans of World War II, and the Shriners. He served as the potentate for the Murat Temple (Indianapolis) in 1956 and as the general counsel of the Shrine of North America in 1969.[8] He also served on the board of Westview Hospital. Steers died on November 30, 1992, in Indianapolis.

NOTES

CHAPTER 1

1. Frank and Edith Richman Papers, private collection (hereafter cited as Richman Papers).

2. Elizabeth R. Osborn, "Indiana Courts and Lawyers, 1816–2004," in *The History of Indiana Law*, David J. Bodenhamer and Hon. Randall T. Shepard, eds. (Athens: Ohio University Press, 2006), 257–77.

3. *Chicago Herald-American*, March 15, 1940.

4. Frank N. Richman, "A 'Majority of the Electors' Means a Majority of Those Voting on the Question," *Indiana Law Journal* 9, no. 7 (April 1934): 403–33.

5. *In re Todd*, 208 Ind. 168, 193 N.E. 865 (1935).

6. The 1970 judicial amendment to the Indiana Constitution changed the way state supreme court justices are chosen. Effective January 1, 1972, they are nominated by a judicial nominating commission and appointed by the governor without regard to political affiliation and subject to approval or rejection by the electorate every ten years. The amendment also eliminated the district residency requirement.

7. James H. Madison, *Indiana through Tradition and Change: A History of the Hoosier State and Its People, 1920–1945* (Indianapolis: Indiana Historical Society, 1982).

8. Madison, *Indiana through Tradition and Change*, 400; *Tucker v. State*, 218 Ind. 614, 35 N.E.2d 270 (1941).

9. *Tucker*, 35 N.E.2d at 305.

10. Ibid., 313.

11. *Liberty Mutual Insurance Co. v. Stitzle*, 220 Ind. 180, 41 N.E.2d 133 (1942).

12. *Kizer v. Hazelett*, 221 Ind. 575, 49 N.E.2d 543 (1943); *Hoesel v. Cain, Kahler v. Cain*, 222 Ind. 330, 53 N.E.2d 769 (1943).

13. *Morris v. Buchanan*, 220 Ind. 510, 44 N.E.2d 166 (1942).

14. *Nash Engineering Co. v. Marcy Realty Corp.*, 222 Ind. 396, 54 N.E.2d 263 (1944).

15. *Indiana Harbor Belt Railroad Co. v. Jones*, 220 Ind. 139, 41 N.E.2d 361 (1941).

16. *Indianapolis Star*, June 13, 1946.

17. *State ex rel. v. Montgomery Circuit Court*, 223 Ind. 476, 62 N.E.2d 149 (1945).

18. *Indianapolis Star*, June 13, 1946.

19. *Indianapolis Times*, June 13, 1946.

20. Ibid.

21. Frank Richman, undated speech, Richman Papers.

CHAPTER 2

1. For information on Shake's background, see John Barnhart and Donald F. Carmony, *Indiana: From Frontier to Industrial Commonwealth*, 4 vols. (New York: Lewis Historical Publishing, 1954): 3:20–21; Knox County, Indiana, Biographies, "Curtis Grover Shake," http://members.tripod.com/~debmurray/indybios/knoxbioref-2.htm#cshake.

2. Curtis G. Shake Papers, Byron R. Lewis Historical Collection Library, Vincennes University, Vincennes, IN (hereafter cited as Shake Papers).

3. Curtis G. Shake, interview by Thomas Krasean and Robert Montgomery, April 10, 1968, Vincennes, IN, transcript, Indiana State Library, Indiana Division, Oral History Project, Indianapolis, IN.

4. Curtis G. Shake, "The Higher Duty" (class oration, Indiana University, Bloomington, IN, June 20, 1910), Shake Papers.

5. Shake to Jake Gimbel, January 1, 1938, Shake Papers.

6. Shake interview.

7. Ibid.

8. Ibid.

9. Shake interview.

10. *Indianapolis Star*, April 14, 1927.

11. *Indianapolis Times*, April 14, 1927.

12. Shake to George L. Saunders, April 16, 1927, Shake Papers.

13. Shake to Charles C. Benjamin, May 3, 1927, ibid.

14. *Shelbyville Democrat*, September 29, 1928.

15. *Shelbyville Republican*, October 8, 1928.

16. *Fort Wayne News-Sentinel*, October 23, 1928.

17. Ibid., October 24, 1928.

18. *Indianapolis News*, November 3, 1928.

19. Ibid.

20. *Indianapolis Star*, November 3, 1928.

21. *Columbus Republican*, November 3, 1928.

22. *Vincennes Commercial*, November 4, 1928.

23. *Decatur Democrat*, November 1, 1928.

24. Shake interview.

25. Shake to Governor M. Clifford Townsend, December 12, 1937, Shake Papers.

26. Shake interview.

27. *Warren v. Indiana Telephone Company*, 217 Ind. 93, 26 N.E.2d 399 (1940).

28. *Warren*, 26 N.E.2d at 108–110.

29. *Helms v. American Security Co.*, 216 Ind. 1, 22 N.E.2d 822 (1939).

30. *Railway Express Agency v. Bonnell*, 218 Ind. 607, 33 N.E.2d 980 (1941).

31. *Heiny, Admx. v. Pennsylvania Railroad Co.*, 221 Ind. 367, 47 N.E.2d 145 (1942).

32. Shake interview.

CHAPTER 3

1. Harvey Fireside, *The Nuremberg Nazi War Crimes Trial* (Berkeley Heights, NJ: Enslow, 2000), 29.

2. *New York Times*, February 2, 1947.

3. In Edith Richman's diary entry for June 11, 1947, she recounts General Taylor's wife showing her a newspaper clipping about how "college girls calling themselves 'War Widows of World War III' were picketing the White House demanding that Federal Judges be sent to Nürnberg to the trials." Edith kept a daily diary for almost the entire time that the family lived in Nuremberg. Frank Richman also occasionally kept a diary during the same period. Both diaries are part of the Frank and Edith Richman Papers.

4. Richman to Julian Sharpnack, February 8, 1947, Frank and Edith Richman Papers, private collection (hereafter cited as Richman Papers).

5. Edith Richman diary entry, February 24, 1947.

6. Ibid., March 1, 1947.

7. Ibid., March 3, 1947.

8. Ibid., March 19, 1947.

9. Ibid., March 27, 1947.

10. Frank Richman diary entry, March 18, 1947.

11. *New York Times*, April 20, 1947.

12. *New York Times*, February 9, 1947; L. M. Stallbaumer, "Frederick Flick's Opportunism and Expediency," *Dimensions* 13, no. 2 (1999), http://www.adl.org/Braun/dim_13_2_flick.asp.

13. *The New Yorker*, December 13, 1947.

14. Frank Richman diary entry, March 25, 1947.

15. Ibid., March 26, 1947.

16. Ibid., April 9, 1947.

17. Frank N. Richman, "Highlights of the Nurnberg Trials," 7 F.R.D. 581 (1947).

18. F. N. Richman, "The Nurnberg Trials . . . seen by an Alumnus," *Lake Forest College Alumni Bulletin* (February 1950): 3.

19. Richman, "Highlights of the Nurnberg Trials."

20. Frank Richman, undated speech, Richman Papers.

21. *New York Times*, April 20, 1947.

22. Richman undated speech.

23. Ibid.

24. "Trials of War Criminals before the Nuernberg Military Tribunals under Control Council Law No. 10, Nuernberg October 1946–April 1947, Volume VI: The Flick Case, Military Tribunal IV, Case 5" (Washington, D.C.: U.S. Government Printing Office, 1952), http://www.mazel.org/NMT-HOME.htm.

25. John Alan Appleman, "Case No. 5 (Flick Case—Industrialists)," in *Military Tribunals and International Crimes* (Indianapolis: Bobbs-Merrill, 1954), 171–75.

26. Christopher Simpson, *The Splendid Blond Beast: Money, Law, and Genocide in the Twentieth Century* (New York: Grove Press, 1993), 379n.

27. Ibid., 271.

28. "Trials of War Criminals before the Nuernberg Military Tribunals under Control Council Law No. 10, Nuernberg October 1946–April 1947, Volume VI: The Flick Case."

29. *New York Times*, December 19, 1947.

30. "Trials of War Criminals before the Nuernberg Military Tribunals under Control Council Law No. 10, Nuernberg October 1946–April 1947, Volume VI: The Flick Case."

31. Richman undated speech.

32. Richman, "Nurnberg Trials . . . seen by an Alumnus."

33. Appleman, "Case No. 5 (Flick Case—Industrialists)," 174.

34. Simpson, *Splendid Blond Beast*, 270.

35. Richman undated speech.

36. Ibid.

37. Ibid.

38. Frank Richman diary entry in Edith Richman's diary, September 24, 1947.

39. Ibid., September 26, 27, 1947.

40. Edith Richman diary entry, October 28, 1947.

41. Ibid., December 8, 1947.

42. Ibid., December 18, 1947.

43. Richman undated speech.

Chapter 4

1. Curtis G. Shake, speech (Vincennes Historical and Antiquarian Society, Vincennes, IN, May 14, 1968).

2. Ibid.

3. Curtis Shake to Mary Alice and Gilbert Shake, July 30, 1947, Curtis G. Shake Papers, Byron R. Lewis Historical Collection Library, Vincennes University, Vincennes, IN (hereafter cited as Shake Papers).

4. Ibid.

5. Shake speech.

6. Curtis G. Shake, interview by Thomas Krasean and Robert Montgomery, April 10, 1968, Vincennes, IN, transcript, Indiana State Library, Indiana Division, Oral History Project, Indianapolis, IN.

7. Ibid.

8. *The New Yorker*, December 27, 1947.

9. Shake speech.

10. *The New Yorker*, December 27, 1947.

11. Josiah E. DuBois Jr., *The Devil's Chemists: 24 Conspirators of the International Farben Cartel Who Manufacture Wars* (Boston: Beacon Press, 1952), 69.

12. *The New Yorker*, December 27, 1947.

13. "Trials of War Criminals before the Nuernberg Military Tribunals under Control Council Law No. 10, Nuernberg October 1946–April 1947, Volume VII: The Farben Case, Military Tribunal VI, Case 6" (Washington, DC: U.S. Government Printing Office, 1952), http://www.mazel.org/NMT-HOME.htm.

14. Ibid.

15. Ibid.

16. Ibid.

17. Joseph Borkin, *The Crime and Punishment of I. G. Farben* (New York: Free Press, 1978), 138.

18. Raymond G. Stokes, *Divide and Prosper: The Heirs of I. G. Farben under Allied Authority, 1945–1951* (Berkeley: University of California Press, 1988), 29.

19. Shake speech.

20. *New York Times*, August 29, 1947.

21. Shake speech.

22. DuBois, *Devil's Chemists*, 82.

23. Ibid., 95–96.

24. Borkin, *Crime and Punishment of I. G. Farben*, 145–49.

25. DuBois, *Devil's Chemists*, 342.

26. Borkin, *Crime and Punishment of I. G. Farben*, 150.

27. Ibid., 151.

28. Ibid., 153–54.

29. *The Nation*, August 14, 1948.

30. DuBois, *Devil's Chemists*, 339.

31. Ibid., 347.

32. Borkin, *Crime and Punishment of I. G. Farben*, 149.

33. DuBois, *Devil's Chemists*, 355.

34. Robert E. Conot, *Justice at Nuremberg* (New York: Carroll and Graf, 1983), 517.

35. Stokes, *Divide and Prosper*, 153.

36. Frank M. Buscher, *The U.S. War Crimes Trial Program in Germany, 1946–1955* (New York: Greenwood Press, 1989), 64.

37. "Very Strange Indeed," *Prevent World War III*, November–December 1948, p. 36.

38. *Indianapolis Star*, November 12, 1948.

39. Shake to Drew Pearson, November 12, 1948, Shake Papers.

40. Ibid.

41. DuBois, *Devil's Chemists*, 356.

42. Shake to Pearson, January 26, 1960, Shake Papers.

43. Shake to Ross Garrigus, May 10, 1948, ibid.

44. Shake speech.

45. *Indianapolis Star*, December 12, 1948.

46. *Harrisburgh (PA)Telescope-Messenger*, January 8, 1949.

47. Shake to Lilly von Schnitzler, March 27, 1950, Shake Papers.

48. About twenty years after the war, it came out that, while in Paris, Achenbach had been intimately involved in arranging the deportation of Jews to the concentration camps.

49. Ernst Achenbach to Ambassador Robert D. Murphy, September 14, 1949, Shake Papers.

50. Josiah E. DuBois Jr. to Shake, July 7, 1952, ibid.

51. Shake to James Morris, January 20, 1961, James Morris Collection, Series 10154, State Archives and Historical Research Library, State Historical Society of North Dakota, Bismarck, ND.

52. *Vincennes Sun-Commercial*, January 22, 1961.

53. Shake interview.

54. Ibid.

55. Ibid.

Chapter 5

1. Remarks of Julian Sharpnack at Indiana University School of Law, Bloomington, IN, November 7, 1952, Frank and Edith Richman Papers, private collection (hereafter cited as Richman Papers).

2. Resolution of Bartholomew County, IN, Bar Association, May 1, 1956, ibid.

3. Yandell C. Cline, speech (Rotary Club, Columbus, IN, April 30, 1956), ibid.

4. Resolution of the Faculty of Indiana University, Bloomington, 1956, ibid.

5. *Vincennes Sun-Commercial*, January 24, 1973.

6. Ibid.

7. *Indianapolis Star*, May 12, 1976.

8. *Vincennes Valley Advance*, September 12, 1978.

9. Ibid.

10. *Vincennes Valley Advance*, September 19, 1978.

11. *Indianapolis Star*, September 14, 1978.

Appendix

1. Bill D. Jackson, *The First Century: Kahn, Dees, Donovan & Kahn, LLP*, http://www.kddk.com/100years/Eville¬_Bus_feature.pdf, 48.

2. *Evansville Press*, January 19, 1992.

3. Mike Magan, "Never a Dull Moment," *The Indiana Lawyer* 8, no. 3 (May 14–27, 1997): 13.

4. "Military Agency Records: War Crimes Records," The National Archives, http://www.archives.gov/research/holocaust/finding-aid/military/
rg-238.html.

5. *Indianapolis News*, February 27, 1946.

6. *Indianapolis Star*, June 2, 1960.

7. *Indianapolis News*, September 11, 1963.

8. Ibid., September 4, 1969.

BIBLIOGRAPHY

PRIMARY SOURCES

James Morris Collection. State Archives and Historical Research Library, State Historical Society of North Dakota, Bismarck, ND.

Frank N. and Edith Richman Papers. Private Collection.

Curtis G. Shake Papers. Indiana State Library, Indianapolis, IN.

———. Byron R. Lewis Historical Collection Library, Vincennes University, Vincennes, IN.

"Trials of War Criminals before the Nuernberg Military Tribunals under Control Council Law No. 10" (Washington, D.C.: U.S. Government Printing Office, 1952), http://www.mazal.org/NMT-HOME.htm.

SECONDARY SOURCES

"Administrative Law: Review by Certiorari in Indiana." *Indiana Law Journal* 16, no. 4 (April 1941): 397–402.

Appleman, John Alan. *Military Tribunals and International Crimes*. Indianapolis: Bobbs-Merrill, 1954.

Barnhart, John, and Donald F. Carmony. *Indiana: From Frontier to Industrial Commonwealth*. 4 vols. New York: Lewis Historical Publishing, 1954.

Borkin, Joseph. *The Crime and Punishment of I. G. Farben*. New York: Free Press, 1952.

Buscher, Frank M. *The U.S. War Crimes Trial Program in Germany, 1946–1955*. New York: Greenwood Press, 1989.

Conot, Robert E. *Justice at Nuremberg*. New York: Carroll and Graf, 1983.

DuBois, Josiah E., Jr. *The Devil's Chemists: 24 Conspirators of the International Farben Cartel Who Manufacture Wars*. In collaboration with Edward Johnson. Boston: Beacon Press, 1952.

Ferencz, Benjamin B. *Less than Slaves: Jewish Forced Labor and the Quest for Compensation*. Cambridge, MA: Harvard University Press, 1979.

Fireside, Harvey. *The Nuremberg Nazi War Crimes Trial*. Berkeley Heights, NJ: Enslow, 2000.

"Indiana Law and Legislation: 1940–1945." Special issues, *Indiana Law Journal* 21, no. 2 (January 1946) and no. 3 (April 1946).

Jeffreys, Diarmuid. *Hell's Cartel: I.G. Farben and the Making of Hitler's War Machine.* New York: Metropolitan Books, 2008.

Knox County, Indiana, Biographies. "Curtis Grover Shake." http://members.tripod .com/~debmurray/indybios/knoxbioref-2.htm#cshake.

Madison, James H. *Indiana through Tradition and Change: A History of the Hoosier State and Its People, 1920–1945.* Indianapolis: Indiana Historical Society, 1982.

Oddi, Marcia J. "Maintaining the Balance of Power between the Legislative and Executive Branches of Indiana State Government Post-1941" (October 26, 2003). http://www.indianalawblog.com/documents/FINAL_10260.

Simpson, Christopher. *The Splendid Blond Beast: Money, Law, and Genocide in the Twentieth Century.* New York: Grove Press, 1993.

Stallbaumer, L. M. "Frederick Flick's Opportunism and Expediency," *Dimensions* 13, no. 2 (1999). http://www.adl.org/Braun/dim_13_2_flick.asp.

Stokes, Raymond G. *Divide and Prosper: The Heirs of I. G. Farben under Allied Authority, 1945–1951.* Berkeley: University of California Press, 1988.

Withered, Jerome L. *Hoosier Justice: A History of the Supreme Court of Indiana.* Indianapolis, 1998.

INDEX